Life Lines

Life Lines

An Introduction to Palmistry

PETER WEST

quantum

LONDON • NEW YORK • TORONTO • SYDNEY

quantum

An imprint of W. Foulsham & Co. Ltd.

The Publishing House, Bennetts Close,
Cippenham, Slough, Berkshire, SL1 5AP, England.

ISBN 0-572-02412-6

Copyright © 1998 Pentagon

Printed in Great Britain by St Edmundsbury Press Ltd, Bury St Edmunds, Suffolk

Contents

Introduction 7

1 Hand Prints 11

2 Hand Shapes 15

3 The Fingers 23

4 The Mounts 35

5 The Thumb 43

6 The Back of the Hand 49

7 The Lines of the Hand 55

8 The Head Line 63

9 The Life Line 71

10 The Heart Line 77

11 The Fate Line 81

12 The Minor Lines 85

13 Special Marks 93

14 Dating Systems 101

15 Dermatoglyphics: The Fingers 105

16 Dermatoglyphics: The Palmar Patterns 115

17 Gesture 121

Index 127

Introduction

The hand is a dazzling complexity of fat, bone, muscle, ligaments, tendons and exceptionally sensitive nerve endings. With it we communicate. We construct, play, love, heal and direct with the hand and, in so doing, express ourselves in a thousand different ways.

The hand is a direct servant of the mind, obeying its instructions in an instant. Reflex action reverses this situation: the mind becomes the servant of the hand. Therefore, it is safe to assume that personality is involved in such actions.

The hands are employed for so many different exercises that defined traits of character become associated with them – much in the same way that we adopt a particular stance or gesture when walking, so that we can be recognised even at a distance. In communication, therefore, the hand is of prime importance. There is a constant interaction between the hand and the mind, forming a continuous flow of information.

One consequence of this interactive communication is that the hand adopts a particular and recognisable shape. And such definable forms have been carefully categorised to indicate specific personality traits, the study of which is known as palmistry or chirology.

Palmistry is divided into three distinct branches which make up the whole: *chirognomy,* the study of the shape of the hand; *chiromancy,* the study of the palmar features, particularly the lines; and *dermatoglyphics,* which involves the skin patterns of the fingers and the palmar surface. It is imperative that none of these features should be used as the basis of an analysis without taking into account the other two factors.

The shape of the hand may be interpreted as being an indication of the basic personality, which rarely changes once the mature mind adopts its chosen path through life. Circumstances which drastically alter the lifestyle have been known to alter the shape of the hand and this will be reflected in the lines on either or both of the hands.

The lines are a reflection of a person's mental and

emotional approach to life and can alter daily. Lines will change with fluctuations in health and at times of emotional or mental stress. Should the effects of such variations leave a deep impression on the personality, they will leave a mark somewhere in the hand.

It is this particular aspect of palmistry that has suffered most throughout history because it has been associated with simple fortune telling and the 'black' arts. But the advances made in palmistry over the past fifty years or so invalidate simple superstition and place this study in a respectable and acceptable category as a reliable method of assessment.

Dermatoglyphics, the name given to the study of the skin patterns, is basically a genetic and biological effect shown in the hands. The patterns are established in the womb and never alter. They reveal a basic attitude towards life which influences the shape of the hand and this, in turn, affects the lines which will indicate how such potential is being applied.

A common error is to look at the lines on the hand without proper reference to the hand's shape and without taking the message of the skin patterns into account. There is a golden rule of palmistry: *no single feature, however strong it may appear, should ever be taken in isolation.* Always check for supportive evidence elsewhere in the hand before stating conclusions.

The skin patterns, therefore, indicate the basic attitude to life and help to colour the features shown by the hand shape. The lines reveal how this potential is utilised and interpreted. But there is a further element of character assessment that many chirologists employ, and that is gesture.

We rarely communicate our ideas without illustrating them with our hands to some extent. This trait is ably demonstrated when someone is asked to give directions, pleads a cause, defends an action or is under pressure. Even at rest or play, we all display recognisable gestures which clearly indicate our moods or intentions. Most of these are habit, but some are deliberate, and we shall study these as we progress.

Palmistry may be used for a variety of reasons: it can determine character, inherent talent, disposition and potential. Its use as a means of vocational guidance is, therefore, unparalleled: a square peg can be taken from its round hole and placed where it will do most good. The days when a son or daughter had to follow their parents are long gone, particularly when it can be chirologically proven that they would be better off following a career for which they have more talent.

Health variations may be detected long after and before their occurrence because the hand indicates not only where the trouble may lie, and its cause; it can also point to the correct way to better health. The study of hands is utilised in various diagnostic work. For example, the hand prints of newborn babies are taken in order to verify whether there are congenital irregularities present which are not otherwise physically recognisable. Psychologists observe hand gesture in their work, and many use basic chirology when determining the probable causes of mental illness and the best way to tackle the healing process. Also, some organic diseases can be detected in the hand and, if found in time, curative steps can be taken. In such cases, prints of the hand taken at regular intervals indicate the rate of progress.

Such a process is not only rewarding to observe, it is also a further step towards the unification of science and mysticism. Palmistry has long been considered a mystic art when, in fact, it is a valuable and precise method of qualifying and quantifying all aspects of human potential.

1

Hand Prints

No serious study of the hand should be undertaken
without reference to hand prints. For a brief
observation, limited by time and convenience, a reading
of the hand itself can yield a great deal of information. However,
hand prints not only provide a more permanent reference, they
are much easier and more convenient for a prolonged study
that may last several hours broken into three or four sessions.

The hand is covered with tiny capillary lines and influence
markings which are not normally visible, even with the aid of a
good magnifying glass, but these become apparent and more
easily readable on a print of the hand. There are two reasons for
taking such prints. If properly taken, the print will record
everything and will form a reference piece which can be
referred to at any time, whether the subject is available or not.
Furthermore, as time goes by, a series of prints taken at regular
intervals will record changes as an improvement or a worsening
of a condition occurs.

There is some information regarding the physical hand that
will not be recorded on a print, such as nail information, colour
and texture. This should be recorded either on the back of the
print or, alternatively, on a record card and filed away for future
reference and cross-indexing purposes. In a short while, a small
reference library of prints will provide many hours of enjoyment
and help to build up experience. In the event of a client
contacting the palmist at a later date for follow-up information
or for a new consultation, the whole history of the subject is to

hand and readily available and will give the client the impression of an efficient office and a friendly, personal service.

Materials

The requirements for taking prints are simple. You will need a small 10 cm/4 in roller, such as is used in photography, and a small sheet of plate glass about 30 cm/12 in square. White glossy paper is ideal although, if there is no watermark, photocopying paper can be used. An ordinary wooden kitchen rolling pin at least 4–5 cm/1½–2 in in diameter and a tube of black, water-based lino ink come next. Fingerprint ink may be used but it is messy and difficult to clean from the hands. Water-based ink will simply wash straight off if the hands are held for a few moments under a cold, running tap and afterwards washed in warm, soapy water. This is an important point: cold water closes the pores so that the hand can be cleaned more quickly; washing in warm or hot water opens the pores and the ink will be far more difficult to remove.

Method

The method of taking hand prints is simple and a few practice runs will result in expert prints. Squeeze about 2.5 cm/1 in of the ink on to the glass. Roll out the ink until it is of an even consistency. Ink the hand gently but firmly with the roller, remembering to take in the outer edges, the fingertips and at least 4 cm/1½ in of wrist below the hand in order to ensure that the rascettes are clearly recorded.

Your subject should be seated comfortably at a table, preferably with a small cloth or ordinary towel covering the smooth surface. Place a sheet of blank paper over the roller with the bottom edge of the sheet just touching the table nearest the subject. Place his or her wrist on the paper and roll the hand evenly back towards the body.

A couple of trial runs should provide sufficient practice. Not much pressure will be required, but care should be taken to ensure that the fingertips and thumb print out properly. If you hold the top edge of the paper as the print is completed, the hand can be lifted from the paper in a nice flowing motion in order to prevent smudging.

It is possible to take up to four prints of each hand without re-inking. Wash the hands and the equipment under cold running water, then finish off with warm, soapy water.

It is not always possible to use this method of taking prints, however, for a variety of reasons. The elderly may suffer from rheumatism or arthritis, or your subject may have an injury or temporary problem which means this first method cannot be used. And, of course, you may not have the necessary equipment with you.

Alternative Method

Assuming that you do have your equipment but that there is a physical problem that cannot be overcome, the following alternative method is as good as the previous one, but needs a little more care and attention to produce good working prints.

Ink the hand as before. Place a small, folded cloth on the table and lay the paper on this. Ask your subject to relax the hand as fully as possible: this can be easily achieved by getting him or her to give a limp shake of the hand from the wrist.

Place the hand squarely on the paper, ensuring that the subject does not move it once it is in place. Press the back of the hand lightly at the fingertips, the wrist, the sides and particularly in the centre of the palm. Hold the corners of the paper and ask your subject to lift their hand straight up from the paper: never take the paper from the hand.

Some palmists suggest outlining the hand while it rests on the paper because it does give an idea of the shape of the hand at a later date. In practice, I find this misleading because it draws attention away from the palm during examination; also, the subject is quite likely to move their hand or fingers and smudge the print. Finally, a small card should be attached to the back of the print on which the following information should be detailed:

1. Colour, skin texture
2. Nails
3. Knotting and flexibility
4. General description of the back of the hand
5. Peculiarities

It is preferable to write nothing on the front of the print as this will ensure uniformity of appearance as your collection of prints in enlarged. Also, reference or cross-indexing will supply any necessary additional information without causing any distraction when you are looking at the prints. It is surprising how often you will go through the prints for fresh information, how much more you will discover and how often little things you had not previously noticed will come to light. Finally, of course, studying the prints will add to your powers of detection, observation and analysis.

In an emergency it is possible to make do with lipstick, a stamp-pad or even the contents of a child's paintbox in order to take hand prints. However, whatever you use, even as a temporary measure, do remember that you are making a mirror image of the palmar surface: a hand print with the thumb appearing on the left-hand side of the palm is that of the right hand.

Whether examining an actual hand or a print you should obtain a good-sized magnifying glass, a watch-maker's eyepiece or, if possible, the type of glass used by fingerprint experts and stamp collectors. This last item is absolutely essential for intensive close work and enables even the most minute detail of the skin pattern to be closely observed comfortably without undue strain. A metric ruler, a small pair of pointers, a notebook and a pencil will complete your equipment.

The Golden Rule

No single feature in the hand should be taken in isolation as an adequate indication of character. Each facet of personality revealed by examination must be assessed in the light of each and every other factor. Only if this is done properly can accuracy be ensured.

The left hand will always indicate hereditary traits: gifts, talents, leanings and implications. The right hand will show how far these interest have been developed, if at all.

Both hands should always be read in conjunction with each other.

Now you are ready to read your first pair of hands.

2

Hand Shapes

The hand can be regarded as a map of an unexplored country. It will have all the ingredients of a normal map: borders, contours, hills and vales, etc. A fine network of roadways – the lines – traverse this imaginary country and, in order to establish the significance of the roads, we have to assess the terrain on which they appear.

Although the lines generally retain the same basic meaning, they do take on a different emphasis according to the type of area they cross. The relative strengths and weaknesses of the lines, therefore, often have to be adapted to the ground (hand) on which they are found.

This is invariably the weak point for aspiring hand readers. It takes time to learn to assess correctly the basic type of hand because there are seven in traditional palmistry. However, for the sake of simplicity, we shall only refer to two basic hand shapes: the square, rectangular or useful; and the conic, round or artistic. All other hand shapes are, in fact, variations on these two themes.

So, when first looking at the hand, it is most important to establish its shape: is it square or round?

This may not be easy since, somewhat confusingly, the hand may often appear to be one shape when viewed from the back and quite the reverse when it is turned over. Therefore, be sure to always assess the shape of the hand when looking at the palmar side. If it looks square, oblong or rectangular on the palmar side, that is the basis from which you start. Almost invariably, most hands will seem to have a squarish shape,

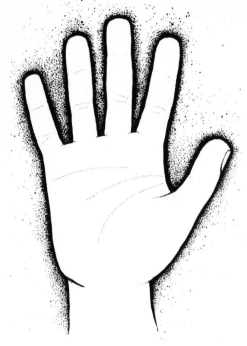

Figure 1

THE SQUARE HAND

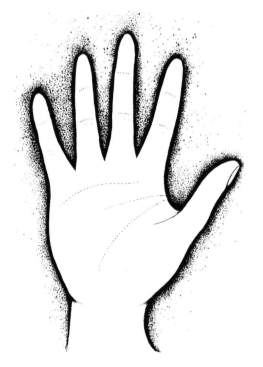

Figure 2

THE CONIC HAND

irrespective of the fingers, when it is viewed from the back.

The Square Hand

The square hand looks exactly that. The edges of the hand appear fairly straight and the base of the hand at the wrist has a straightish appearance. The top of the palm can be quite different, however, because the fingers may be evenly set, or the first finger or the little finger, or both, may be lower. Also the fingers may be long or short, thick or thin, straight or crooked. But if the whole hand, including the fingers, presents an even picture, the hand should be classified as square.

Square, or utilitarian, hands are found everywhere: in all types of communities, business concerns and industries. People with this hand shape hold conventional views and somewhat fixed opinions and tend to have great respect for law and order. They are basically practical folk who can literally turn their hands to all kinds of useful tasks.

Such subjects are orderly, methodical and logical, often irritatingly so because they love reason and tend to regard with suspicion anything new and untried. Philosophy, other than the homespun variety, has little or no place in their world.

Square-handed types have endless patience, are level-headed but can be determined and very stubborn if they so choose. They rarely demonstrate acts of affection in public – almost looking over their shoulders to see if anyone is looking. As a general rule, square hands have few lines on the palms.

The Conic Hand

The conic, or round, hand is artistic in almost every sense. Its overall appearance is rounded and tapering fingers with clearly-defined, rounded tips often complete the picture. The edges of the hand have a softer appearance than the square and the outer edges frequently show a definite bulge.

Impulsive and versatile, creative and idealistic, conic-handed folk make and break relationships easily. This is not because they are unfeeling in any way but because they tend to be constantly on the move, always looking for fresh, stimulating contacts. Such subjects care little for old things: it is the new, the untried, that fascinates and they will try anything once. Their knowledge may tend to be superficial, enabling them to converse on many differing and widely varying subjects but without the greater depth of knowledge of the true student. But, to be fair, such folk will make great efforts to find further information on any subject that catches their imagination.

Often the life and soul of the party, conic-handed subjects are popular with all who come within their sphere. Impressionable and very changeable, often inherently lazy, they can display a selfish desire for their own personal comforts. Yet, curiously enough, they will also give you their last penny to help you out of a tight squeeze.

These folk are very moody, strongly imaginative and quite philosophical when things go wrong, quickly bouncing back full of charm and confidence again.

Variations

A square palm may have square fingers that are short in relation to the palm. Equally, the fingers can be long and tapering, straight or crooked, with or without a certain type of spacing. Similarly, a conic palm can have a variety of finger types and all such variations have to be taken into account and must be accurately identified. All these variations have meanings and these differences must be carefully assessed, judged and balanced before conclusions are drawn.

In rare instances, the subject may even have a square left hand and a conic right. Also, of course, there are variations on these two basic hand shapes.

Elementary Hands

The elementary hand is so-called because, once seen, it immediately implies a basic personality. However, one should not jump to the conclusion that people with this type of hand are as simple as the term implies!

The elementary hand is short and clumsy-looking; the fingers may be short and stubby, and the nails badly kept.

People with this type of hand are slow and advanced thinking is not usually their forte. However, their approach to life is instinctive and they are content to leave well alone anything which they do not fully understand.

Yet such people usually have a far better knowledge and understanding of nature than the more intellectually inclined. Basically sound honest folk, elementary-handed subjects usually have contented, well-adjusted personalities.

Figure 3

**THE ELEMENTARY
HAND**

Philosophic Hands

The philosophic hand is long, bony and easily recognisable by the 'knotting' of the finger joints: defined bulges appear at each of the phalanges. The hand is often long and rectangular in appearance with elongated nail phalanges.

Figure 4

**THE PHILOSOPHIC
HAND**

Philosophic-handed people are deep thinkers: studious, ascetic and refined. Sensitive, dignified and proud, they may seem unapproachable and difficult to understand. These subjects care very little for mundane worldly matters: they just want to be left alone and often become engrossed in worlds of their own creation.

Spatulate Hands

The spatulate hand can be a slight variation of the conic or the square. Instead of being totally square in appearance, the hand is broader at the wrist or at the upper part where the fingers join the palm. Often the fingers are wide-tipped at the nail end and have a spatulate appearance.

The basic characteristic associated with people with spatulate hands is extreme restlessness. Activity is their forte because they are highly strung, excitable and full of energy. They are innovative and very independent, sometimes to extremes. They neither think nor act conventionally and are often regarded, unfairly, as cranks. These subjects tend to take short cuts to achieve their aims and, in so doing, sometimes break or bend a few rules into the bargain. They rarely hurt others in the process and little harm is done; however, it is this trait that earns the spatulate-handed people their 'cranky' label if and when things go wrong.

Professional people with spatulate hands are often the inventors in their particular field, although such a hand shape can be found in all walks of life. If the spatulation is widest at the

Figure 5

**THE SPATULATE
HAND**

base of the hand, the subject is usually very active mentally but if it is at the fingers, he or she is more practical as a rule.

Psychic Hands

In direct contrast to the spatulate hand is the psychic hand, which is identified by long, narrow palms and slender fingers tapering to a point with beautifully-kept almond nails. Owners of such hands live in a state of almost total mental and emotional idealism and are completely at a loss in normal society.

These subjects display no practical or business sense and are trusting – too trusting. They tend to confide in the wrong people for the wrong reasons and are easily hurt as a result. Unfortunately, they do not seem to learn by these mistakes and often repeat the whole sorry process over and over again. Idealistic and visionary, psychic-handed individuals are best off living as far away as possible from the madding crowd.

Figure 6

THE PSYCHIC HAND

Mixed Hands

The last of the hand shapes is probably the most common and the most difficult to interpret: the mixed hand. This hand is literally mixed and can take various forms. The palm may be square, one finger spatulate, another pointed, another conic and so on; it may consist of any combination of the available shapes.

Mixed-handed folk are adaptable to any circumstances and rarely suffer at the hands of others. Life is eventful and full of interest to such subjects and they do not have time to become bored or fed-up.

They are very changeable and rarely have a definite goal in sight for very long although they may display one particular characteristic the majority of the time. For example, they may be inveterate gamblers despite the realisation that they could not cope with all the pressures of fame and changed circumstances which a big win would bring. Yet these people will pursue their goals with fanaticism. The successful small businessman often has mixed hands. Such an individual will become highly successful because of his ability to anticipate and adapt to whatever trends occur in his particular field of interest.

3

The Fingers

The four fingers are strong indicators in their own right because they signify the instinctive facets of the subject's personality, whereas the palm represents the more practical aspects of their nature. Individually and collectively their appearance, development, shape and position should be observed from the front and the back. The inclination of one finger to another, and towards other parts of the hand, is also important in assessment.

Finger length, in relation to the palm, is another significant factor. If this relationship is not obvious, the following method of clarification can be used.

Take a ruler and measure the medius finger from its tip to where it joins the top of the palm. Next, measure the palm from the top rascette to the same point. If the finger is longer than the palm, the fingers may be classified as long; if the palm is longer, the fingers are considered short.

If the length is approximately equal, give or take an inch or a centimetre or two, it denotes a nicely balanced personality. More often than not, however, fingers are either long or short in proportion to the palm. They may be smooth or knotted at the joints; conic, spatulate or pointed at the tips; or they can be thick or thin. Individual phalanges, too, may be long, short, thick or thin and the knuckles at the back of the hand should be checked to see if they are prominent or flat.

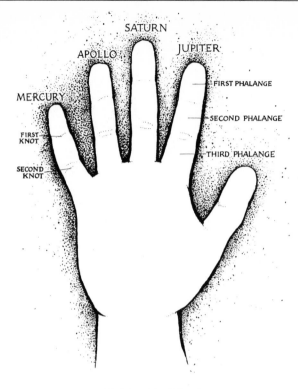

SATURN

APOLLO

JUPITER

FIRST PHALANGE

MERCURY

SECOND PHALANGE

FIRST
KNOT

THIRD PHALANGE

SECOND
KNOT

Figure 7   **THE FINGERS**

Smooth Fingers

Smooth fingers denote versatile, adaptable and intuitive personalities. If also short, their owners will tend to see the plan or scheme before them as a whole and, often, commence a project without completely appreciating the details involved. Consequently, an hour, day, week or month later, they will have turned their minds to a new idea altogether, having been defeated by those details which they did not take into account at first glance.

Conversely, people with long fingers take the time necessary to consider and to assimilate all the information they need before proceeding with a new and unfamiliar task. By taking their time, of course, they are more aware of any potential pitfalls in their course of action, although this does not mean that their approach is necessarily more methodical.

Knotting

A knotting, or prominence, at the joints may be regarded as acting as a stop, or check, in the flow of ideas. Knotting of the top joint denotes a critical nature: someone who will consider all the minor details and finer points not normally taken into account by others in carrying out a simple task.

Knots on the first joints tend to indicate slow, difficult-to-please personalities. Such subjects often worry unnecessarily and are prone to nervous tension. At interviews, for example, they may give poor performances in spite of a first-class knowledge of the subject in hand.

When the lower joints are prominent, this process is taken a step further, and thought and action become very methodical and basic. Tidy, orderly and pragmatic, these people exhibit good self-discipline, suffer less inner tension and rarely give way to emotional displays. They tend to have little imagination and do well in jobs requiring a practical approach.

The knotting of both joints denotes the true sceptic: cold, calculating, precise and logical. These people are best left alone to pursue their own interests, which often take the form of research requiring both intellectual and practical application as they will follow an idea through to the bitter end, no matter how long it takes. Obsessively neat and tidy, such subjects prefer quiet studious surroundings and can be very difficult to live with.

Knuckles

The knuckles are the third joints of the fingers and refer to personal hygiene, general appearance and health matters. If they all appear relatively even, the subject will always look neat and tidy, but may also be a trifle fastidious. Some concern with diet, fitness and personal discipline is almost always present with such a formation.

People with uneven knuckles usually display an outward appearance of orderliness. Often the medius knuckle is most prominent and, when it is, only superficial attention may be paid to personal habits, hygiene and possessions: a room may look neat and tidy, but open a drawer, or lift a cushion! Such subjects may also be a little forgetful in small matters and a regular pantomime will be gone through when searching for a match or looking for money to buy something.

The Individual Fingers

Although individual fingers can be delineated phalange by phalange, it is important always to consider each phalange in relation to those on the other fingers as well as those on the same finger. There may, for example, be a predominance of long second or third phalanges, they may all be short and stubby, the nail sections may have differing tips, even the nails may have differing appearances, and all these formations should be considered in conjunction with other features.

The following is a complete study of the individual fingers, followed by other general observations.

The Index Finger

1st phalange:

Long	*Intuitive. Good judgements made on first impressions.*
Short	*Materialistic, and little faith in human nature.*
Thick	*Sensual, egotistic, inclined to selfishness.*
Thin	*Conventional, can be austere.*

2nd phalange:

Long	*Materialistic, but positive and constructive.*
Short	*Ambition is usually lacking.*
Thick	*A love of comforts and pleasures.*
Thin	*Very ambitious: must not be held back.*

3rd phalange:

Long	*Dictatorial and proud.*
Short	*Uncomplicated approach to mundane matters.*
Thick	*Sexual and sensual; can be greedy and egotistic.*
Thin	*Aesthetic; prim and proper.*

A prominent first joint indicates scepticism, whereas a prominent second joint denotes good self-discipline. When the knuckle is prominent, personal tidiness is indicated.

If the first finger is shorter than the third, the subject can be cold and hard, dislike personal restrictions and react quite violently to any form of criticism or opposition.

A first finger that is longer than the third indicates ambition, pride and plenty of self-confidence. A supple finger-tip denotes versatility; stiff fingertips indicate stubbornness.

When the tip is conic or round, the subject is likely to be intuitive and impressionable; but if square, they will be more conventional: someone who may be a disciplinarian but who has good practical leadership qualities. A spatulate tip indicates a natural leader, an active personality who must be in the forefront at almost any cost.

When the first finger stands well away from the second, the accent is on independent thinking. These subjects, wherever possible, lead their own way of life. If the index finger is close to the middle finger, it indicates a more conventional personality, one who is content to remain 'one of the herd'.

A straight finger reveals an efficient, confident approach; a slightly bent finger indicates a more cautious nature. People with this latter formation are not very trusting souls, particularly if their pride is at stake.

The index finger represents the ego, pride and the ambitious side of the nature. It is the 'I' of the personality: the ruler, leader and guide. As the first indication of character on the radial or conscious side of the hand, it is an important pointer to a person's physical reactions once the mental assessments have been completed.

The Medius Finger

1st phalange:

Long	*Prudent; slightly superstitious; lacking humour.*
Short	*A calm, steady nature and submissive personality.*
Thick	*A lack of stability and refinement.*
Thin	*Sceptical and untrusting.*

2nd phalange:

Long	*A love of the countryside and nature.*
Short	*Rarely learns by experience; can be a wastrel.*
Thick	*Practical; often likes outdoor activities such as gardening.*
Thin	*Scientifically inclined.*

3rd phalange:

Long	*Selfish and unreliable.*
Short	*A frugal, sometimes miserly, nature.*
Thick	*Sociable, but cautious and serious.*
Thin	*Unsociable; a lone wolf.*

A prominent first joint will help to counterbalance the natural tendencies denoted by the finger. A prominent second joint implies that the qualities of the finger will be applied practically. Orderliness and organisation in the home and business and towards personal possessions is indicated by a prominent knuckle.

An over-long middle finger denotes a tendency towards solitude and such subjects may well be of a melancholic nature, constantly searching for the truth.

When of average length (slightly longer than the third finger), a well-balanced attitude to spiritual, moral and mundane affairs is indicated.

A middle and third finger of the same length denotes an unbalanced attitude in business matters. Such subjects are unlikely to prosper for long because of the unnecessary risks which they take.

A conic, or round, fingertip implies a less than serious approach to life; a pointed tip denotes ready optimism; and a square tip indicates a subject who is a strict disciplinarian and profound moralist. A spatulate tip shows an inclination to solitude on the part of the owner, sometimes to the point of austerity combined with pessimism.

However, a supple tip would moderate any of the above qualities and such subjects take a lighter look at life when they choose, whereas a stiff tip would reflect a stiff and unyielding but highly moral nature.

A straight finger denotes a constant awareness of responsibilities. If it leans towards the third finger, the owners are probably unhappy with their lot and tend to feel that the world owes them a living. But a person whose middle finger leans towards the first finger will have a more realistic attitude towards ambition.

The medius is the finger of balance: the midway point between the radial or actively conscious side and the ulna or passive side of the hand. It is normally the longest finger, but when it is not, shortcomings in the character will normally be indicated elsewhere in the hand. These weaknesses almost always manifest themselves in a lack of responsibility to ordinary commitments.

The Annular Finger

1st phalange:
Long	*Artistic, creative personality but, if over-long, a poseur.*
Short	*Lack of artistic and literary ability.*
Thick	*A practical, rather than idealistic, interest in the arts.*
Thin	*Idealistic artistic leaning; a bit of a purist.*

2nd phalange:
Long	*Inspired artistic ability.*
Short	*Little or no artistic appreciation or ability.*
Thick	*Practical creativity; a realist.*
Thin	*Little interest in form, colour or texture.*

3rd phalange:
Long	*Materialistic and often avaricious.*
Short	*Absence of practical application in artistic matters.*
Thick	*Poor artistic judgement, but comfort-loving.*
Thin	*Self-sufficient.*

A prominent first joint indicates critical tastes in artistic matters; a prominent second joint denotes a strong sense of form and design ability. The sort of person who can add two or three lines to a drawing and totally transform it usually has a prominent knuckle on this finger.

If the third finger is over-long, the subject possesses strong artistic and creative leanings, often with a noticeable talent in a particular field of the arts and, sometimes, a tendency towards gambling.

If it is longer than the first finger, it denotes an innate personal happiness and some form of creative ability.

But a third finger that is shorter than the first finger indicates a pessimistic personality. Such subjects are of a non-artistic nature and not usually very creative. They rarely appreciate any form of art.

A conic, or rounded, tip to the third finger shows artistic talent, even if such talent is not used to the full. A pointed tip denotes the born idealist: a highly impressionable dreamer who lacks stability. A square-tipped finger shows an artistic ability and a strong love of comfort and riches. The sure mark of the entertainer is a spatulate fingertip.

A supple tip is indicative of acting ability, good interpretative powers and the ability to be physically creative; a stiff tip, however, denotes a restrictive attitude towards the arts and poor critical values.

When the finger is straight, it will emphasize all those qualities shown by the individual sections. If it leans towards the second finger, business ability will prevail over artistic appreciation, although both traits may be combined to make money. However, when the third finger leans towards the fourth, the subject may display an almost fanatical dedication to acquiring money through art.

The third finger signifies the artistic aspects of life and links practicality with a sense of realism and pure art appreciation. Its development indicates the degree of these traits and both hands must be compared very carefully to see what changes, if any, have taken place.

The Auricular Finger
1st phalange:

Long	*Eloquent, studious, investigative, perceptive.*
Short	*Difficulty in self-expression; mentally lazy.*
Thick	*Poor perception; rather simple mental approach.*
Thin	*Good self-expression; business ability, charm and tact.*

2nd phalange:

Long	Practical; commercial/industrial capabilities.
Short	Unenterprising but loyal employee.
Thick	Business acumen; possible lack of scruples.
Thin	Financially astute; commercial planning ability.

3rd phalange:

Long	Persuasive and eloquent; tendency toward self-deception.
Short	Guileless nature; gullible and lacking perception.
Thick	Poor moral qualities; blatant and vain.
Thin	Unimaginative; no real zest for living.

If the first knot is prominent, it denotes good orderly self-expression; a prominent second joint indicates a precise approach to commercial matters and an instinctive caution which enables the subject to avoid business disasters. A prominent knuckle shows instinctive tidiness: these people cannot tolerate clutter.

A long little finger is one that reaches at least half-way up the nail phalange of the Apollo finger. These subjects have a good command of language, possibly linguistic ability, and enjoy expressing themselves. A short finger implies poor self-expression and a low-set one indicates a lack of self-confidence. Such people will not push themselves forward: they are happy to make up a crowd, but rarely display initiative.

A conic, or rounded, tip emphasizes the subject's ability to express humour. Usually the tip of the little finger is pointed, revealing a ready wit and a balanced sense of humour; the more pointed it is, the more mischievous that humour can be.

A spatulate tip is the mark of the real craftsman: someone who is creative yet practical and can make really difficult tasks appear easy.

The square-tipped little finger denotes a dual nature. These subjects make very good teachers because they can translate theory into practice; they also possess business acumen.

A supple tip emphasizes the subject's mental and aural powers, whereas a stiff tip denotes rigid adherence to accepted principles. Folk with flexible tips are more socially adventurous than those with stiff-tipped little fingers.

A little finger that curves in towards the Apollo shows the individual's instinctive ability to resolve the problems of others. Such people 'feel' their way into the confidence of others and, having done so, are able to correct the relevant troubles in a practical manner.

If this finger stands away from the third, it reveals an individualistic personality. These subjects do not follow the herd and like to act independently.

The auricular, or little, finger lies on the ulna or unconscious side of the hand and indicates how the subject uses the instinctive aspects of his or her nature in ordinary everyday affairs.

Overall Classification

The fingers should be classified together after they have been studied individually. In practice, only four basic types are usually seen: the pointed, square, conic and spatulate.

When all the tips are pointed, it indicates much idealism, which will be tempered by realism if knotting is also apparent. Square-tipped fingers denote more conventional, practical and useful personalities. When round, or conic, tips predominate they refer to good receptivity of ideas, midway between the idealism and practicality of the pointed and square.

Spatulate fingers signify action: these people rarely keep still and must always find something to do with their hands or mind. Youngsters, especially, should be kept busy because, if allowed, they will soon become difficult to restrain and discipline.

Small bulges or 'droplets' sometimes show quite clearly on the palmar side of the fingertips. These signify a highly developed sense of touch and emphasize any emotional extremes of temperament. Subjects with this formation usually display an instinctive and developed sense of refinement.

Ideally, these sensitivity pads should appear on all the fingers, as a set, but they are sometimes found on only one or two fingers. If this is the case, they will emphasize the better qualities of the fingers on which they appear.

Sensitivity pads seem to be associated with special gifts. The nature of such a gift will vary according to the reading of the individual finger on which it is found. Also, it will manifest itself in a different manner according to its setting on the finger: if the centre of the pad is high, the gift will be to do with mental powers; if low, it will be revealed practically; and if centrally placed, this gift will manifest itself in a balance of both.

Setting

The set of the fingers on the palm should be taken into consideration. Evenly-set fingers denote a well-balanced nature although, in practice, the index and little fingers usually appear to be set lower than the middle and third fingers,

If the little finger is set very low, it indicates an inferiority complex stemming from the subject's conviction that he or she is inadequate in some way. Such people tend to shun social life and pick their friends very carefully because of their difficulty in expressing emotional desires in a physical way.

A low-set index finger denotes a lack of self-confidence which will be revealed in the subject's general approach to life. These people are frightened of 'putting on a show' and refrain from pushing forward their own ideas, or those of others.

When both these fingers are set low on the hand, it indicates a lack of positiveness and a great need for reciprocal affection. Such people are very easily hurt.

Spacing

If the space between the first and second fingers is wide, it denotes a confident and self-sufficient personality. These people can be a law unto themselves and will not allow too much interference in their lives.

Conversely, if this space is narrow, the owner is likely to prefer to stay with the crowd and go along with the wishes of the majority.

A wide space between the second and third fingers shows a lack of forethought. Long-term planning does not concern such people, day-to-day existence is all they worry about. If the space is narrow, however, the subject will always keep tomorrow and personal security firmly in mind, and act accordingly.

A wide space between the third and the fourth implies people who will instinctively act on their own, cannot abide vacillation, prefer their own company and must retain their individual identity. A narrow space between these two fingers denotes a dependency on others. These people need constant reassurance in all matters; they tend to ape the ideas and actions of others and are very sensitive to atmosphere.

Definite gaps in the basal phalanges when the fingers are held closed always denote some sort of inadequacy of diet. If the fingers are thin, frugality is implied; if short and thick, overeating and poor diet are the probable causes.

If all the fingers are stiff and unbending, it is likely that the subject's general attitude will be the same. But when they are all flexible, the overall picture is one of general friendliness: someone who is good-natured, eager to please and easily pleased.

4

The Mounts

The mounts are fleshy pads on the palmar surface below the fingers and basal phalange of the thumb; at the base of the hand above the wrist; and the raised section at the percussion, or outside edge of the palm. The extent of the development of the mounts indicates how much the subjects use their natural characteristics.

One formation that should be included in this section is the creative curve. This is usually dealt with in relation to hand shapes, but it more properly belongs to the mounts.

With reference to the digital mounts (Jupiter, Saturn, Apollo and Mercury), the more centrally placed they are below the finger, the better the relevant qualities may be expressed, irrespective of their size. To establish the centre, find the apex of the skin pattern in the mount. Usually this will tend to be slightly off-centre for it is rarely found exactly under the finger. The Mercury mount, for example, nearly always lies to the middle of the hand.

Creative Curve

Often there is a bulge at the top, middle or base of the outer percussion edge of the hand. This formation is unmistakable because it appears as a definite curve and may stretch from beneath the Mercury finger right down to the wrist.

A full curve shows creative energies, often quite original in concept. The subject will have the ability to improve on an idea, or be able to formulate schemes, plans and projects.

If the curve is more pronounced at the top of the palm, the creativity will be mainly inspirational or intellectual; if in the middle of the palm, the subject will have the ability to follow these concepts through and apply them practically. A creative curve towards the bottom of the palm denotes greater practicality. Such people are able to put the plans of others into a concrete form.

A straight edge to the palm denotes a lack of creativity and a tendency to be unable to adapt to new ideas and plans easily.

The Jupiter Mount

When normally developed, this mount denotes pride and ambition, social sense and religious disposition, but if over-developed, it implies arrogance, tyranny, bigotry and selfishness. An underdeveloped Jupiter mount indicates a lack of personal pride and ambition. Such subjects are likely to possess little sense of personal dignity; they may lack respect for authority and tend towards idleness.

The Saturn Mount

This mount, when normally developed, denotes a cautious but balanced attitude towards life, although subjects tend to be over-sensitive. If overdeveloped, it refers to a gloomier nature, a love of solitude or, in some cases, morbidity. When it is quite flat, the person will lack sparkle, decisiveness and humour.

The Apollo Mount

When developed normally, it implies artistic leaning, grace and charm of manner and love of beauty. But overdevelopment denotes greed, extravagance and arrogance. As a rule, subjects with underdeveloped Apollo mounts are basically materialistic, and lack refinement and aesthetic values.

The Mercury Mount

If this mount is normally developed, the subject's perceptive self-expression and commercial ability are usually well marked.

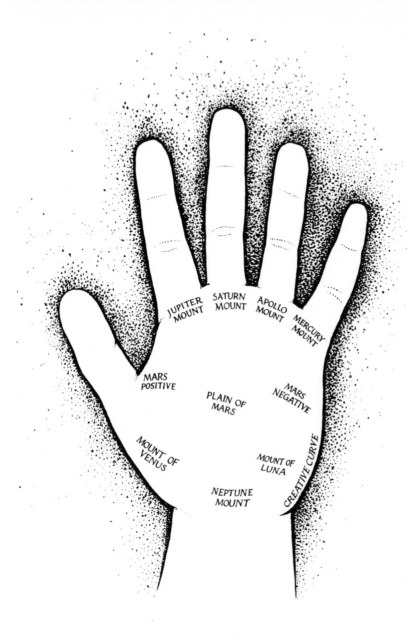

Figure 8   **THE PALMAR MOUNTS**

But when it is overdeveloped, cunning, deceit and outright pretentiousness may be displayed. Underdevelopment implies little or no business ability, poor written and verbal self-expression: an unenterprising personality.

The Mount of the Moon

The Luna mount has special significance owing to its size, the area it covers and the important lines that may cross it.

When fully and obviously developed, it reveals imagination, a love of peace and harmony and a desire to accept, and to be accepted by, all levels of society. These subjects often display restlessness and are attracted by travel. They possess a desire to please, but not at any price; they are attracted to philosophy and mysticism and are mentally sensitive and imaginative.

A flat, lifeless-looking mount implies poor imagination. Such subjects lack sparkle, flair and the ability to communicate their own ideas. Often, their social sense is poor and they may attempt to imitate the more gifted, sometimes with tragic results because they cannot improvise successfully.

The Zone of Mars

Traditionally, there are three areas of Mars: the mount of Mars Negative, Mars Positive and the plain of Mars. Because of their position on the palm, these formations are important and I prefer to read the whole section as one area, or zone.

The zone of Mars stretches right across the centre of the palm from the percussion, or unconscious side, to the conscious and active side, the radial. Major lines cross this area and it is essential, therefore, to establish exactly what kind of terrain they traverse. It is important, however, to look at the other mounts below the fingers before attempting to interpret the nature of the Martial areas because if these are well developed the zone may look flat and underdeveloped.

In order to establish the development of the zone of Mars, the area *must* be tested by touch. Using your finger and thumb, feel the exact depth and fullness of the three sections, especially the plain which, although it may appear flat and uninteresting, may well be the exact reverse. If the area feels firm and springy, it is developed no matter what the eye may see; if it feels thin and bony, then it is underdeveloped.

A developed zone denotes considerable interest in social affairs, even active participation in them. If the positive mount is developed, it indicates plenty of physical and moral courage and a well developed mount refers to social consciousness, perhaps even active participation in political matters. These people will desire and obtain positions of influence or power in local affairs, and gain satisfaction from using their talents in these areas.

A developed negative mount denotes determination and staying power. Adverse situations will only challenge these people to utilise their abilities to win through, even in what may be almost permanent uphill struggles. This formation is often seen in the hands of the disabled who may have to fight the world in order to be allowed to lead as normal a life as they can without outside help. So, be sure of your ground if you see this sort of development because you will certainly need your wits about you!

Should any, or all, of these areas be underdeveloped, it lessens the interest shown in world affairs. It implies the type of people who read the same paper every day, make a verbal comment but cannot take the problem further, even if they know their opinion is the correct one: in their estimation the fight simply isn't worth it. These subjects do not lack moral fibre, but cannot visualise or initiate practical methods of changing adverse situations.

This particular area is often, mistakenly, seriously neglected. In traditional palmistry, a flat appearance to the zone of Mars is known as a 'hollow' palm and is interpreted as being unlucky. Nothing could be further from the truth, however, as any luck will result from the owner's own actions or lack of them and correct counselling could overcome any potential problems.

The Mount of Neptune

Full and developed mounts signify sparkling personalities. These magnetic qualities will be emphasized if the life line ends on the mount of Neptune or if the fate line begins there. These folk display a clearly defined ability to communicate at all levels and others feel at ease with them because of their compassionate and understanding natures. Such subjects have an unerring instinct for deciding on the correct course of action in any situation. But a flat and hollow mount denotes subjects who are quite indifferent to other people and to the world in general.

The Mount of Venus

Strictly speaking, this is not a mount in the pure sense, but the third phalange of the thumb. Yet, in both Western and Oriental palmistry, it was and still is considered to be the most important mount in the hand. Indian and Egyptian palmistry especially credited this mount with such importance that complete books have been written about it.

This area – bounded by the life line, the line of vitality – is the seat of basic emotions, the quality of affections, libido, family relationships and physical energies. It should, therefore, be carefully assessed in relation to other parts of the hand at all times although, in this chapter, I shall treat it purely as a mount.

When full and developed, with a minimum of lines, it shows a capacity to live life to the full, to enjoy physically the day-to-day existence. If firm to the touch, it indicates a love of the outdoors, sporting interests, good libido and a healthy attitude.

A soft full mount implies that physical pleasures will dominate. A fine tracery of lines across the mount will add excess to any selfish or immoral characteristics here.

But a firm lined mount indicates that the natural instincts will be under reasonable control, although there could be occasional lapses. The subject is likely to be warm-natured, instinctive and tender, fond of the arts and good company.

A low or poorly developed mount denotes a certain coldness, perhaps even an inability to love. Such folk often have little regard to the feelings of others and can be selfish. Having no sensitivity, they have little or no appreciation of art. For these people, everything must have a use or be a means to an end and this will be apparent in their attitude to those around them.

The development of this mount also refers to the subject's home life and inter-family relationships, both in respect of their childhood home and the one they currently occupy. Full and healthy-looking Venus mounts denote a good, well managed home with a warm welcome for all who visit it. Conversely, under-development implies that the home is regarded merely as a place where one lives: warmth will be lacking in such cases and hospitality inclined to be frugal to the point of mere civility.

Horizontal lines that cross the Venus mount from the family ring and run through the life line always show some form of family interference in the subject's lifestyle. Vertical lines indicate that the subject has made efforts to improve his or her domestic circumstances. If these lines also cross the line of life, this indicates some degree of success, depending on their length and termination. A fate line that starts on the Venus mount, inside the life line, usually refers to a business or career associated with the family.

Placement

On some hands, the mounts merge or one mount leans towards another. When this occurs it is important to establish which mount is displaced because this will colour the interpretation of the second mount. For example, if the Jupiter mount encroaches on to the Saturn mount, the Saturn mount will reflect some of the Jupiterian qualities.

Sometimes, the Venus mount appears to be pushing the Luna mount to one side, and this indicates an excess of physical energy; but poor self-discipline is indicated if the Luna pushes the Venus mount over. The Neptune mount lies between these two mounts; therefore, it may be safely assumed that the imagination of such subjects will strongly affect their emotions and intensify their reactions to such an extent that they may live in a state of almost constant fantasy. But, if all three mounts are flat, their owner may have difficulty in registering precise and logical ideas concerning life and, if this lack of mount development is combined with poor lines, the subject is likely to conduct their life by almost always 'muddling through'.

5

The Thumb

The thumb is the key to the personality. Essentially a human characteristic, it is known as the signature of the hand and represents will-power, reason, logic, vitality, behaviour and direction of purpose. In Eastern palmistry it is considered of paramount importance, even to the extent of negating the 'golden rule'.

Extreme care should be taken in judging the abilities shown by the thumb because the left and right thumbs frequently differ, if only very slightly. The thumb should be observed in relation not only to the rest of the hand, but also to the other hand and thumb. For example, a strong left thumb may have a weak right partner, or vice versa.

The left hand is representative of natural talents, while the right indicates whether such gifts have been developed or not. A strong right thumb, therefore, indicates a strong character: one that has developed for reasons that will be clearly shown elsewhere in the hands. A strong left, with a weak right hand, may refer to progress which may be impeded by circumstances, ignorance or unwillingness to go forward.

Simply looking at the thumbs before starting a detailed analysis will reveal a lot of information. They should always look as if they 'belong' to the hand: a huge thumb which dwarfs the rest of the hand may be just as out of place as a tiny appendage that looks like an afterthought.

The length of the thumb should be roughly equivalent to that of the little finger or, if held close to the index, it should come at least half-way up the third phalange. It should look strong enough for the hand and, when relaxed, the angle between the thumb and the index finger should be between 45° and 90°.

Angle

The wider the angle the more self-reliant the subject will be. Usually, the thumb makes an angle of between 60° and 90° to the index, denoting good discipline, directed will-power and a sensible application of logic and reason. When this angle is narrow, it implies a lack of responsibility, poor will-power and weak reasoning abilities.

A very narrow angle, less than 45°, indicates a tendency towards selfishness, small-mindedness and prejudice. These people have limited intelligence, poor perception, limited responses and are slow to exert their will-power. A very wide angle, greater than 90°, denotes very different characteristics. Such people display a sense of responsibility and leadership qualities most of the time. However they are still capable of foolhardy action and will take a chance, or stop at nothing to gain their own way in the end. It is the mark of the hero, dead or alive.

Phalange Length

Ideally, the nail phalange of the thumb which indicates will-power should be the same length as the second which relates to logic. When the phalanges are of equal length, which is quite rare, it indicates a well-balanced, self-contained personality, who is very well suited to positions of authority. These people know the secret of how to blend power with initiative, responsibility with action.

When the first phalange dominates, so does determined action, often at the expense of diplomacy and reason. In such cases it is often a matter of 'I want – I will have'. If the second phalange is the longer, discipline is not so well marked and work tends to be done in fits and starts. Although rational, perceptive and intelligent, these subjects are poor starters and require supervision to keep them on their toes.

The Tips

Conic, or rounded, tips to the thumb indicate emotionally-orientated individuals who react quickly to external stimuli. More idealistic, hesitant and indecisive are subjects with pointed thumb tips. They are impressionable, quick to solve problems and to spot weaknesses in the defences of others.

A square-tipped thumb denotes the realist. These people are open to reason and, although they can be hard taskmasters, they lead by example, rarely asking others to do things they cannot or will not do themselves.

The spatulate tip is the sign of the craftsman. Impulsive perhaps, these instinctive personalities get things done.

The spoke-shaved tip describes a flat-topped thumb which, when viewed from the side, tapers more and more as it reaches the tip. People with this formation have a special ability to get others to do things for them which they would not ordinarily do even if, afterwards, they question their motives! The spoke-shaved tip is often mistaken for a pointed tip, but the owner of the former is more diplomatic than the latter.

A bulbous top to the thumb indicates basic appetites. Such folk are passionate and obstinate, capable of blind fury if opposed, lack refinement and are ruthless in pursuit of an aim. If the tip of the thumb bends outwards, it denotes a streak of generosity and open-mindedness but, if it turns inwards, the owner may be acquisitive, selfish, mean and petty.

Flexibility

Supple thumbs indicate an impulsive nature. These folk may appear weak but should never be underestimated because they can be all things to all men. Mean one day, generous the next, they have a tendency to vary their everyday lives in order to offset boredom.

Stiff-thumbed folk are disciplinarians. Stubborn and unyielding, even when offered a favourable compromise, they can be consistent and persistent workers: very difficult to understand, they are hard to work with, and living with them needs the patience of a saint.

Length

An over-long thumb marks the owner as having an excess of will-power and determination: a love of command is accentuated. Such a person may or may not make a good leader.

Well-balanced phalanges will indicate a good, inspiring manager but an over-long first phalange denotes a tyrannical personality. An over-long second phalange implies that too much time will be spent in reasoning out the problem without enough action being taken. However, once ideas are implemented, any opposition will be swept aside because all the possibilities will have been considered.

Alignment and Setting

When held naturally, the thumb either opposes the fingers or aligns with them. People with opposing thumbs will have great control over their inner feelings, no matter how 'open' their character appears to others. Few, if any, will share the really innermost thoughts of such people and those who do will have to abide by their terms otherwise bitter and unforgiving enmity will result.

It is difficult to know how someone with an opposing thumb may react in a given set of circumstances but, when this is seen,

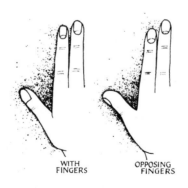

WITH
FINGERS

OPPOSING
FINGERS

Figure 9   **THE ALIGNMENT OF THE THUMBS**

signs of inner conflict will be apparent elsewhere in the hand.

A thumb that is virtually in alignment with the fingers shows a much more enthusiastic and spontaneous personality. Will-power wilts in the face of enjoyment and such subjects will tend to lose themselves in the pursuit of pleasure.

A high-set thumb denotes creative, original ideas and is often associated with a gift for solving problems in unusual ways. A low-set thumb indicates a more inspirational nature: someone who can be sparked off into new ventures by the most minute events.

The Basal Phalange

The basal phalange of the thumb is known as the mount of Venus and is dealt with more fully in the chapter on mounts. But there are one or two important points which should be explained here.

The extent of the development of the mount of Venus is very significant. If the basal phalange is so developed that it is much larger than the first and second phalanges of the thumb, it means that the subject's physical appetites may interfere with normal life even to the extent of causing emotional, sexual, moral and social problems. Conversely, a thin, flat-looking basal phalange often refers to prudery, introversion and a dislike of even discussing what may be politely referred to as 'personal matters'.

The adverse effects of a developed mount on the left hand may be moderated by a smaller version on the right. If this is the case, the subject may be aware of potential personal problems. If the right hand is more developed than the left, any character weakness will be confirmed elsewhere in the palm.

Sometimes the edge of the thumb appears angular rather than curved. Two angles are formed between the wrist and the second phalange and, if these are clearly defined, they refer to a sense of tempo: the lower angle concerns harmony; the upper, rhythm. One may be present without the other, of course. But, if present, they can bestow a sense of rhythm to a dancer or skater for example, or creative flow to a composer or writer.

In the practical rather than creative sense, these angles denote a good sense of timing in social matters. Intellectually, they imply a fluid understanding of everyday life and, sometimes, an interest in the behavioural patterns of people.

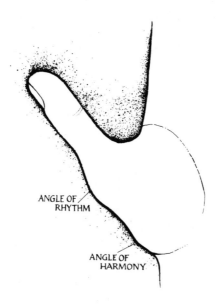

ANGLE OF
RHYTHM

ANGLE OF
HARMONY

Figure 10

THE ANGLES OF RHYTHM AND HARMONY

6

The Back of the Hand

It is possible to examine the backs of the hand at any time: while travelling, from photographs, during recruitment interviews or on a hundred and one other occasions when you are able to notice, assess and draw conclusions.

The back of the hand can provide much useful information. Colour, breadth, length, nails and gesture all reveal facets of the overall personality. The size of the hand in relation to the rest of the body has been the subject of a special study in psychiatry, and gesture, in particular, has been the subject of much research. Different countries and cultures offer different interpretations of gesture although the chapter dealing with this refers only to the results of modern chirological studies.

Probably the first thing we notice, apart from the colour and size of the hand, is the nails.

Nails

Nails are important, for they show temperament and health. However, the tips should not be taken into account for they may be shaped according to fashion and can be misleading. The shape dictated by fashion may have a bearing on the style of life but care should be taken when examining nails from a distance, particularly as the use of coloured nail varnish often prevents in-depth analysis.

Note the appearance or non-existence of moons. If there are no moons on any of the fingers, the subject's health may not be very good. However, moons can 'disappear', implying an

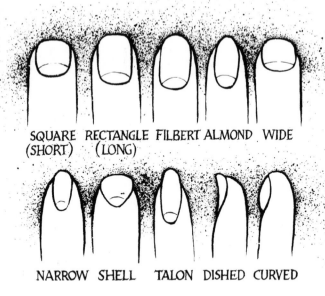

SQUARE RECTANGLE FILBERT ALMOND WIDE
(SHORT)　(LONG)

NARROW SHELL TALON DISHED CURVED

Figure 11　　　　　　**NAIL SHAPES**

early warning of ill health from an organic source. Merely looking will not, therefore, give accurate information: during a personal consultation the subject may or may not be able to clarify the situation.

Good clear moons on all fingers should be regarded as a sign of a good healthy body and a contented mind, chirologically speaking. But, if they are haloed with a bluish tinge, it may indicate a predisposition to vascular troubles.

Nails can be square or rectangular, long or short, filbert- or almond-shaped, talon-like, wide or narrow, shell-shaped, dished or curved. A nice, pale, milky pink is the best colour.

A square end to a nail may emphasize a square-tipped finger but it can also mask a spatulate or pointed tip. Square nails show an unforgiving nature, someone who is slow to anger, but emotional. If deeply coloured, anger may be colourfully expressed but, if pale, beware revenge at a later date. The smaller the square, the smaller the subject's outlook on life is likely to be: narrow-mindedness and a lack of real warmth will prevail and there may also be a degree of self-righteousness.

Filbert nails indicate individuals who are placid and peace-loving. Such people tend to live on their nerves and may not have a lot of physical energy. Slow to anger, they dislike loss of face and sometimes display outbursts of temper which usually upset them more than those whom they oppose.

Rectangular nails also indicate people who are placid by nature, even-tempered and dislike all forms of disturbance in the natural order of things. Concerned with their health, these subjects are fastidious and do not like work that involves getting their hands dirty.

Subjects with almond nails are similar to those with filberts in many ways, but there are some distinctions. Courteous and refined, with sensitive natures, they make devoted and loyal friends and employees. Truthful and basically honest, they are not easily upset but, when they are, they may exhibit hysterical outbursts.

Talon-shaped nails often reflect a poor diet and subsequent bad health. Born survivors, these subjects tend to take what they want when they want it, displaying little finesse or style except for an unvarying assertiveness.

Wide nails indicate those who are quick to anger and equally quick to forget, though not necessarily to forgive. The shell-shaped version shows some degree of nervous or mental exhaustion and indicates recent stress: nature is saying slow down now – or else!

Dished or curved nails refer directly to poor health. Dished nails indicate the probability of a poor blood supply, nutritional deficiency or a glandular problem. Curved nails almost always indicate chest problems such as lung, respiratory or possibly tubercular infection.

The dishing effect usually indicates a deficiency brought about by nervous or mental neglect which attacks the weak points of the system, whereas the curved nail relates directly to any organic weakness in health. Either way, both are indications of potential or actual health problems and remedial action is necessary.

Short nails, whatever their shape, denote criticism, whereas long nails are indicative of greater tolerance on the part of the subject. Bitten nails always refer to poor emotional balance. Irritability, intolerance, introspection and loneliness are the usual contributory factors in such cases.

Longitudinal ridging often accompanies bitten nails, but it also occurs on other nail formations. An inherent chronic problem may be the cause, but it can also be hereditary. In either case, these ridges fade when suitable treatment is given. Horizontal bars or ridging is, however, associated with ill health. The causes may be accidental, infectious, nutritional or the result of emotional shock.

Spotting on the nails is not regarded as serious, except where the spots are white, which could refer to a calcium deficiency. Traditionally, white spots are supposed to refer to love affairs, the finger on which they are found allegedly referring to the partner's character type. On Jupiter, for example, the lover could be a lawyer or teacher, etc. There is no modern justification for this theory, but you may wish to test it yourself.

Nails take approximately 180 days to grow and this is measured from the base of the nail. A barring effect half-way along the nail, which could refer to an illness, would therefore indicate that this had occurred some 2–3 months previously. With experience, you will learn to judge this accurately.

General Appearance

The colour of the hand can indicate the subject's natural qualities. Pale skin, or the white type so beloved by poets of the last century, usually relates to a cold, selfish nature for example. Sun-tanned skin shows a love of the outdoors, although this may be a temporary condition; take a careful look at the rest of the body to ensure that this conclusion is correct. If the skin texture appears rough, then certainly a love of the outdoors is likely and, if it is also a very basic (square) type of hand, the subject may well be a craftsman or labourer. Close examination of the hand shape should indicate whether the owner is a carpenter or engineer, a site surveyor or a sportsman.

Hairiness and texture can also give clues to an individual's nature, although, like skin colour, you should regard these only as guidelines and not as definite statements of fact.

Hair on the back of the hand usually indicates a fairly stable constitution, although not necessarily physical strength as is said in traditional palmistry.

A smooth-textured hand implies a degree of refinement in the subject's general approach to life and a rough texture normally shows someone with a natural, perhaps slightly coarser, attitude.

When the thumb is closed in to the side of the hand, a mount is formed at the junction of the base of the thumb and forefinger. This formation is commonly known as the 'mouse' and is an indicator of health. A firm full mount indicates that the subject's general health and recuperative powers are likely to be good, whereas a flatter, softer formation implies a generally weaker constitution: someone more likely to succumb to viruses, colds, etc.

A firm full mount also denotes a subject with a natural zest for life, someone who enjoys the company of others and life generally. But when low and soft, the opposite applies: such folk rarely seem to get far in life, lack enthusiasm and refrain from joining in.

A wide back to the hand denotes a love of the outdoors, whereas narrow backs refer to less exhilarating habits and hobbies. If the backs of a subject's hands differ widely, it usually denotes that changes have been wrought through circumstances beyond the owner's control. A wide right and narrow left hand shows that the subject has developed their interests; whereas the reverse indicates that something has happened to cause the change. But, in both cases, you can usually trace the root cause by studying the front of the palm.

7

The Lines of the Hand

The majority of people associate the term palmistry solely with the interpretation of the lines on the hand to indicate past, present and future events, although this study is more properly called chiromancy. It is important, therefore, to realise that it is not possible to date such events precisely from the lines in the hand. What is revealed in the palm, however, is the development of personality traits as the subject matures and experiences life.

The constant changing of the lines and smaller influence markings will indicate the changes made, or being made, as the subject's life progresses. The palmist, having established the type of hand being dealt with, must then decipher the meanings of the lines within the context of the hand type on which they appear.

As the subject's character matures, the experienced palmist will be able to pick out past events that have left their mark in the palm and, having reached this point, will be able to interpret present trends. Only after this has been done is it possible to refer to potential future events as shown in the hand.

Implications

Lines should be scrutinised very carefully. Various irregularities are usually present but are not normally visible to the naked eye, so I would recommend that you use a good-sized magnifying-glass. Remember, the left hand denotes inherited and natural

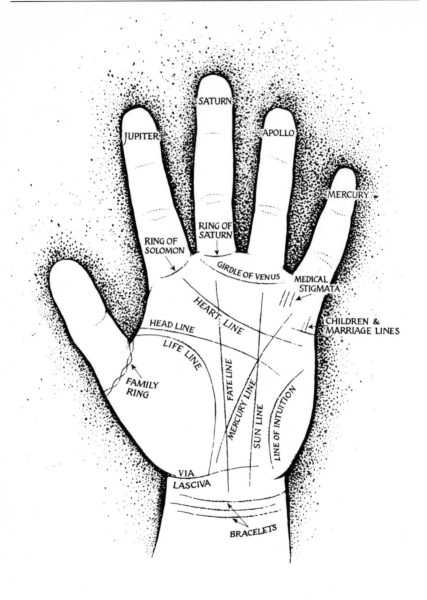

Figure 12   **THE LINES OF THE HAND**

inclinations and refers to talent, ability and the implementation of natural desires. The right hand shows how far these traits have been developed, if at all, and whether or not the subject is happy in his or her current environment. It also reveals whether the current occupation is an extension or manifestation of such talents, natural abilities and desires.

Obvious differences in the two hands show changes in the subject's lifestyle, so you must look to see if these have caused any inner tensions and, if they have, how far they influence the current life situation. As you gain experience of the meanings of the lines, you will learn to detect such changes, their effects on the subject and how much influence remains to cause prejudice or favour.

The right hand is the master and reveals the extent of any development of the natural gifts conferred by the left, even if the subject is left-handed. Similar-looking hands are rare, but the more alike they are, the less change has been needed or desired in the lifestyle.

Clarity

The clearer the lines on the hand appear, the better. They can be likened to wires or cables carrying a current, or a water pipe: wherever an obstruction of any kind appears, the less the natural abilities conferred by the line in question are able to be used properly.

Besides being clear, the lines should be of a depth and strength applicable to the hand in which they are found. Very deep engravings on a pale hand refer to inner conflict, for example, whereas pale or faint lines on a healthy-looking palm imply a jaded constitution which may or may not be temporary. The clearer the path of the line, the more straightforward the personality and the more the natural abilities denoted by that line are utilised by the subject.

Referring back for a moment to the idea of comparing a line with a cable carrying current, we can see that any apparent weakening of the line must inhibit the flow of the current. Or, comparing the line to a water pipe, if the line splits in two and rejoins later, the flow of water has been stopped temporarily:

the normal strength, the natural flow or usual enthusiasm has changed the attitude of the line.

Markings

When a line does divide into an islanded formation, it frequently refers to poor health which will last for as long as the island is present (this is explained more fully in other chapters). A dot on a line indicates a short-term blockage, but a series of dots may refer to a recurring illness.

A cross-bar, or an influence line cutting through the line, denotes a temporary halt in the natural energies, possibly caused by worry or tension. Tasselled or fraying lines indicate such energy is being wasted, although at the end of a line a tassel merely shows the natural decline of the energies through age. Where a line continues its course after this formation, however, it refers to a variety of interests occupying the subject at the point indicated.

Breaks in the lines should always be regarded as warnings. If a break occurs on one hand only, it shows a temporary setback or illness, usually confined within the context of the line on which it appears. But if it appears in both hands, it is a dire warning of an accident, serious ill health or a cessation of the influences denoted by that line.

A break in the life line signifies a termination of the current lifestyle, an accident or ill health. On the head line it indicates an accident, ill health or the end of an old commitment; on the heart line, vascular trouble or possibly the severance of an emotional tie; and, on the fate line, it suggests an end to that particular aspect of the career or a complete change of environment.

There will usually be other markings in the hand leading up to any breaks in the lines and these will give a good indication of the reason for such a break.

Differences

If there is a distinct difference in the head line on each hand, see if the basic hand shape differs. This is often the case where the subject has had to overcome many obstacles in trying to achieve ambitions. Sometimes the subject may even have had to change his or her fundamental beliefs as a result.

In the case of the life lines differing, domestic or environmental circumstances may have caused such changes. If the heart lines differ, emotional problems are often the root cause.

Full and Empty Hands

When observing the lines for the first time, it will be easy to recognise a 'full' or 'empty' hand.

The full hand is one with an amazing network of lines totally covering the palm and making it difficult to see the skin pattern. This is the mark of the worrier, the person with a vivid imagination, emotional and probably highly-strung. Sensitive to a fault, unpredictable, invariably artistic in some way, creative and philosophic, these individuals usually lack self-confidence.

Such subjects seem automatically to distrust the motives of friends and associates, yet are normally willing to give them the benefit of the doubt. They are often basically unhappy owing to their almost constant fear of upsetting others. Indeed, they live on a razor's edge half of the time, just waiting for something to go wrong and, not surprisingly, it does not take long in their view.

Full-handed people are perceptive, but lack initiative; understanding and sometimes quite clever, they rarely achieve distinctive positions in life. Although they shine when in the limelight, they are frustrated in routine jobs. These subjects do not take kindly to discipline, yet may be good at imposing it because they worry so much about the finer details that little will escape them.

These people are often found in positions of authority which they have acquired merely through their ability to impress. However, in the long term their careers may suffer as a result of their lack of continuity of purpose. These individuals are restless and jumpy, ill at ease under pressure and, although good at theory, largely impractical.

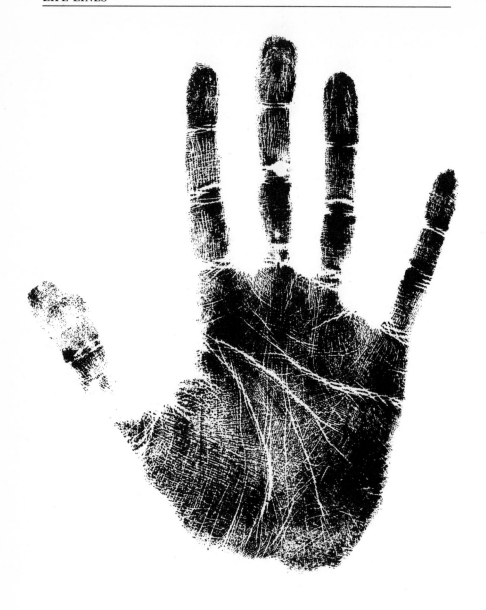

Figure 13   **THE FULL HAND**

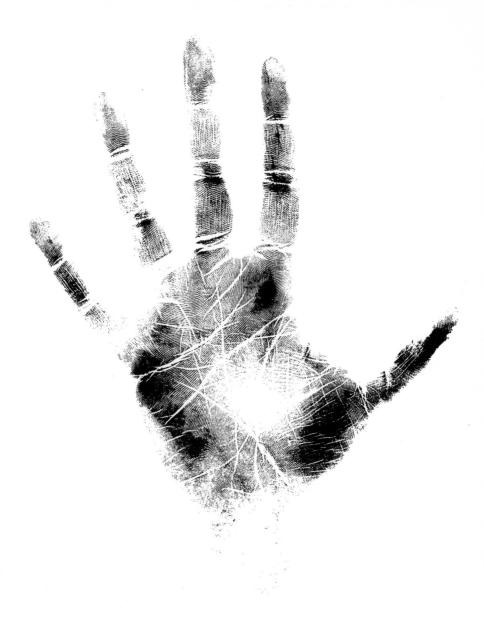

Figure 14   **THE EMPTY HAND**

The empty-handed personality is quite the reverse; with just the basic three or four lines and little or no hint of influence lines, the palm looks empty.

These people do not feel things as acutely as full-handed types and, although they may have deep feelings, rarely show them. They are relatively free from worry and troubles; they tend not to get over-excited and dislike unnecessary emotional involvements. Mentally, these individuals show a great sense of purpose, but lack obvious enthusiasm for a project, however dear it may be to them. They do have feelings, of course, but simply do not show them as much as other people.

Empty-handed subjects may appear unintelligent whereas they are in reality merely slow to react to ideas. Once their minds are made up, however, such people go ahead and do what has to be done, often quite thoroughly. They are not usually overly concerned with politics, world situations or idle chit-chat, but they will, if they decide a cause is worth fighting for, move heaven and earth to redress a balance they feel is wrong.

These people are well suited to jobs in the armed services or a service industry. They observe convention, obey orders, are punctual and orderly. They are straightforward; they lack originality and creativity and go through life quietly and unobtrusively in a routine, orderly fashion.

The Average Hand

It is sometimes difficult to know how to read those hands which fall half-way between full and empty. If the hand looks full of life and is covered by a network of lines, read it as full; if only the basic lines are apparent, classify it as empty. Somewhere between these two lies the hand that is obviously more than an empty palm, but has not enough lines to be classified as a full one. In such a case, a simple check to see if there are more vertical than horizontal lines will give a further clue to the subject's personality.

Generally, vertical lines refer to efforts made towards improving conditions whereas horizontal lines refer to obstructions, either through a lack of self-perception or the interference of others.

8

The Head Line

The head line indicates intellectual capacity and potential. Unlike the line of life, the type of hand on which it appears should be taken into account when identifying the abilities indicated. This line may start anywhere on the Jupiter mount or from the line of life, or inside it, and travel across the plain of Mars, either dipping or sloping slightly or steeply. The head line may fork at or before its termination.

There are many variations to be taken into account when dealing with this particular line which is probably the most important of all the major lines. All relevant features must be noted carefully for this is the line that will tell you how the subject reacts to all external stimuli. Even if the rest of the hand seems to disagree with the message of the head line, this is where you should start your in-depth character analysis – subject to the 'golden rule', of course.

The principal feature to look for is a clear, unbroken line with as few interruptions as possible. However, the head line may appear furry, wavy or straight, islanded or chained; it may be heavy or light in comparison with other lines in the hand.

The Start of the Line

A line that starts on the Jupiter mount, with a clear, easy slope towards the other side of the hand and devoid of too much interference, indicates that the subject will have a good intellect, retentive memory, straightforwardness and well-balanced reasoning powers. The greater the slope, the more the subject's imaginative powers will be brought into play.

The higher the line starts on Jupiter, the more honourable the character, not only in dealings with others but in self-examination also. However, if the line appears heavy in comparison with the rest of the hand, self-satisfaction is likely to be overdone and selfishness or egotism may prevail.

The wider the gap between the head and life lines, the more rash and impulsive the personality. Ambition, leadership, confidence and the ability to carry plans through are the chief characteristics of these people. Unfortunately, these traits sometimes result in antagonising others because tact and diplomacy become an act rather than an art.

The closer the head line starts to the life line, the greater the subject's feelings for other people. If tied to the line of life, impulse is likely to give way to conventionalism and the closer this tie, the more sensitive and emotional the subject's thought processes.

When the head line starts inside the line of life, from the mount of Mars, the general approach is one of caution, owing to a decided lack of confidence. In such cases, subjects often under-employ their mental powers because their emotions rule their intellect.

The Course

A long head line that runs straight across the palm denotes a rational and fixed but somewhat cold nature, particularly if the line is wholly above the centre of the palm. When this line reaches the percussion, the individual's feelings will be subjected to their will and, if the head line actually rises towards the fingers, it implies that all emotion is cut out of any relationship.

Usually, the head line has a sloping or curving appearance. With such a formation, the longer the line, the more developed the creative powers of the owner are likely to be. Too deep a curve to the mount of Luna will, however, indicate an overactive imagination and the deeper this line dips into the mount, the more poorly balanced the intellect.

A short, curved head line denotes a more mundane and less

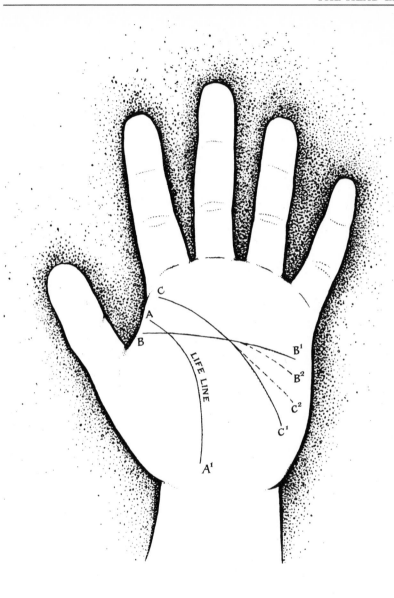

Figure 15   **VARIATIONS OF THE HEAD LINE**

Key

A–A₁   A short straight head line

B–B₁   A head line that cuts the hand in two

B–B₂   Shows how this line may fork to form a 'creative' fork

C–C₁   A long sloping head line. The creative fork touches the outer edge of the hand at C_2 indicating international recognition

65

creative intellect, though the subject's memory will still be good if there is no interference in the line. If the line appears heavy at its start then tails off weakly, it refers to an incident that has caused the subject to stop using his or her mental powers fully; all the abilities are still there, but they are no longer used.

On a square hand, the head line is usually straighter than on a conic or spatulate palm, denoting an orderly and rather conventional mentality. However, when it does curve and slope on a square palm, it indicates someone who is more imaginative and creative. A short, straight head line implies rationality, sometimes accompanied by art appreciation.

Forks

A fork at the end of the line indicates a two-fold talent: creativity is both mental and practical. This formation is sometimes referred to as the 'writer's fork', although its presence does not necessarily imply an ability to write for a living. It does, however, indicate that such subjects are likely to employ their creative talents additionally to their usual career. Indeed, such a person may well follow two jobs or professions concurrently.

If one of the branches touches the outer edge of the palm, it is said to confer international fame on the subjects for their work, although notoriety rather than fame may be the result in a poorly developed hand. A very wide fork implies conflict between the career followed by the subject and their preferred form of self-expression.

This formation invariably denotes an untapped or under-employed talent. Therefore, if it is seen in the hands of children, it is important for the parents to encourage the development of such inherent ability as much as they can.

Duality

Occasionally, a double head line appears in a hand, but rarely in both hands. Such a marking is usually found on the right hand and implies the subject exists in two different worlds simultaneously, often holding two careers that rarely mix. Few will realise that the subject is so gifted because he or she may go to extraordinary lengths to ensure that the two lives do not clash.

A similar situation may arise when the right-hand head line sweeps straight across the palm, effectively cutting the hand in two. Even if this line slopes slightly, it denotes a subject whose mind effectively controls almost all his or her responses, irrespective of other indications in the hand.

Great care should be exercised if this formation is present in a hand because, although warmth and generosity are often denoted by other indications in the hand, the subject's mental strength can override all other feelings. If it is found in both hands, which is rare, the subject's mind will govern all their actions and reactions: emotions will be kept completely under control at all times.

A head line that lies close to the heart line denotes less natural control and the emotional side of the nature may outweigh the intellectual approach. The rest of the hand will indicate the relative strengths of both aspects of the personality.

Appearance

A furry appearance to the head line usually indicates a temporary lack of concentration. Inadequate rest or diet may be the cause or, perhaps, an emotional affair that has got temporarily out of hand.

Influence lines rising from the head line show efforts that have been made to improve circumstances; falling lines denote incidents that have interrupted the owner's ambitious progress.

An island has a weakening effect on the line's power, but this will be restored once the period indicated by the island has passed. Dots on the head line denote a tendency to worry or an inability to think clearly; a tasselled ending indicates that the subject has poor concentration and may be easily distracted from any activity.

A break in the head line is indicative of danger. Traditionally it refers to a head injury and my own findings support this. If a break occurs in this line on both hands, it implies that the mental abilities will be affected by an accident, illness or a breakdown. A square joining the two broken ends will, however, denote some protection: the subject will probably come through such an experience safely, but it will have a lasting effect.

Sometimes a short, straight head line will dip suddenly, often at a point below the middle and third fingers, indicating business ability. Such a practical streak may well enable the subject to convert one profit into a means of acquiring even greater profit. This trait is most likely to be utilised when the dip occurs immediately below the Apollo finger.

When the head line is stronger-looking than the life line, physical activities are likely to be of secondary importance. The head will rule such subjects, who usually display an excess of nervous energy. Sometimes, mental problems may arise owing to the fact that these individuals tend to ignore their physical needs entirely.

The Simian Line

The head line may occasionally be seen to unite with the heart line to form one straight line across the top of the palm. This formation is known as the Simian line and is a sign of great mental energy and emotional intensity.

A line from the Simian line to the life line often signifies a tremendous emotional blow that has completely altered the subject's way of thinking. Even when the effects of this blow become blurred with time, such people's resolve never to be hurt in such a manner again does not fade and they will continue to hide their feelings beneath a 'hard' exterior.

In rare instances the presence of a Simian line may supersede the 'golden rule' and be the overriding factor in interpretation of the hand.

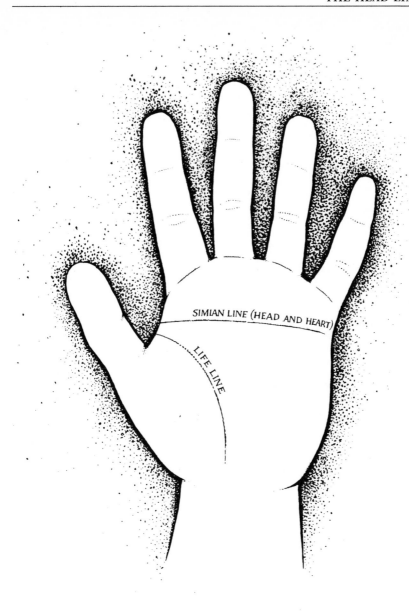

SIMIAN LINE (HEAD AND HEART)

LIFE LINE

Figure 16   **THE SIMIAN LINE**

9

The Life Line

The line of life may start anywhere in the region of the mount of Jupiter or Mars Positive and sweeps out into the palm, encircling the mount of Venus in a firm but gentle curve. It can end anywhere: under the base of the Venus mount; in the middle of the Neptune mount; on Luna; or in the palm, just short of the base of the hand.

The firmer and wider the sweep of this line, the more vitality and zest for living is implied. If it is free from all influence lines, it shows a sound constitution and, should it terminate on the Luna mount as well, it indicates a restless, vigorous, adventurous and 'open' personality.

The life line should be read as an indicator of health and physical well-being. With a full and healthy-looking Venus mount, the owner should be reasonably robust. A poor, weak-looking line reflects a poor health factor.

If this line follows the outer curve of the mount of Venus closely, it implies a restrictive attitude and a lack of physical energy. On a wide palm, this would indicate limited activity, but on a narrow one, it indicates a general lack of enthusiasm for anything, physical or otherwise.

The Start

When the life line starts on the mount of Jupiter, it is a sure sign of ambition and drive towards self-improvement. Usually, however, this line starts below this point, between the mounts of Jupiter and Mars.

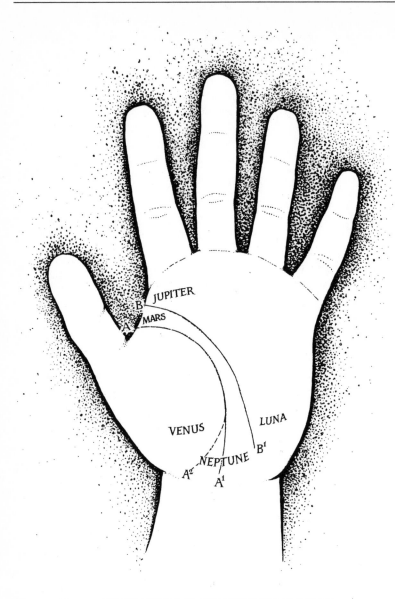

Figure 17   **VARIATIONS OF THE LIFE LINE**

Key

A–A$_1$ A normal life line
A–A$_2$ A 'stay-at-home' life line
B–B$_1$ A restless life line

A line that starts on Mars indicates someone who is slightly reticent and a bit unsure of life. A Jupiter start denotes leadership qualities, but a Mars start shows the opposite.

Sometimes the life line has a poor beginning: it is islanded, or chained, or has little influence lines running in all directions virtually obscuring it at first. This indicates childhood weaknesses such as poor general health or minor illnesses.

If the life line commences with an open island at its very beginning, it indicates some mystery attached to the birth. Traditionally, it refers to illegitimacy, but it may equally well indicate that there was some difficulty involved in the actual birth of the subject.

The Course

The longer the line continues in a chained and islanded fashion, the longer is the period of poor health. Indeed, such a formation may refer to a recurring illness that still affects the subject. Any breaks in, or downward influence lines from, the life line denote interruptions in the good health of the subject.

All upward-reaching lines from the life line's main pathway refer to special efforts made by the subject to further his or her ambitions. Cross-lines from the mount of Venus through to other parts of the palm indicate changes and influences wrought by others, usually adversely. If these cross-lines start from the family ring, they refer to family matters and may indicate the family's disapproval of the subject's chosen way of life. The ends of all these influence lines indicate the particular area of conflict.

If the life line is tied to the head line for a short while at its start, it indicates certain restrictions in the subject's early life. This formation occurs more frequently in the left hand than in the right, indicating that the subject made efforts to become more self-assured during childhood. Such restrictions may refer to problems at school, health weaknesses, parental domination or environmental problems.

When the life line sweeps further into the palm of the right hand than of the left, it denotes a sustained, conscious effort towards greater personal freedom. If the reverse is true, this implies reduced circumstances in which the subject has had to make do with whatever has been available in material and personal terms and is conscious of this problem.

A direct influence line from the main line to a specific area of the hand shows a conscious effort to improve the relevant circumstances. For example, if the influence line goes to the Jupiter mount, it refers to academic or educational ambitions; a line to the Apollo indicates artistic and creative aims.

A wide gap between the head and life lines denotes an incautious attitude, whether conscious or subconscious. The speech and actions of such people are often rash, although no real harm is intended unless otherwise indicated elsewhere in the hand.

The greater the space between the life line and the Venus mount, the more lively the subject's personality is likely to be. Such people recover quickly and well from emotional setbacks and their general attitude to life is warm and generous. However, when the Venus mount is restricted by the life line, discontent and lack of warmth are indicated.

As the line progresses on its downward path, it should appear clear and strong but its termination point can vary considerably. Often, the life line stops half-way down the hand and this may mean that the subject has ceased making any real effort.

Alternatively, it may indicate that life has simply become too difficult and the subject is quite content to live life without further efforts to improve matters.

The Termination of the Line

If the line ends in a distinct fork, the owner is restless, particularly when one of the branches terminates on the mount of Luna, indicating that he or she likes to travel; when the other branch finishes under the ball of the thumb, a strong love of home comforts is indicated.

A life line that ends under the Venus mount in the left hand, but on the Luna mount in the right, indicates a subject who likes to travel but will always wish to return home between times. If, however, the line terminates on Luna in the left and under Venus in the right, the love of travel will be more imaginary, perhaps manifesting itself as a liking for travel books or films. No desire to travel is indicated if the life line terminates under the Venus mount in both hands, but when this line ends on the Luna in both hands, the subject is likely to be a definite wanderer.

Double Lines

Occasionally, there is a 'sister' line just inside the life line on the mount of Venus, sometimes referred to as the line of Mars. This line helps strengthen the characteristics of the life line, whether that line be weak or strong, emphasizing and defining its qualities.

Sometimes two life lines are apparent in the same hand. The original life line may stop soon after it has started and a new, vigorous, strong one develop further into the palm, usually starting from the head line. Careful identification is necessary, however, as a fate line can be mistaken for this second line.

Where this formation is present, it may indicate the subject's total dissatisfaction with his or her home and environment. Such people literally make a new life for themselves, leaving the family home as soon as is practicable, often at the expense of the family or other close relationships, in search of personal freedom. Usually, when they later have children of their own, their offspring are treated far better than they were, although, unfortunately, this sometimes results in a lack of discipline.

Length

One of the more traditional superstitions regarding the life line associates its length with life expectancy, but this is totally incorrect. A short life line does not imply a short life any more than a long life line implies a long life. People can and do exist with a life line that is extremely short, perhaps only 2 cm/¾ in long, or with no life line at all on their hands. Admittedly, such folk may suffer from poor health, but they can and do live to a ripe old age.

There may, of course, be people in their nineties who have extremely long life lines in their hands, without any trace of weakness at the termination points. And, although this does imply a long, healthy life, it is still usual for such elderly people to have a short illness before passing on. Where the line tassels and frays, it shows a general weakening of the constitution as the natural resilience of youth becomes lost; and there may well be a long period of ill health before death.

Breaks

A break in the life line in one hand sometimes refers to an accident or a period of ill health and this is even more likely to be so if a similar break occurs at the same point in the other hand. However, even if the break occurs in both hands, indicating a highly hazardous period for the subject, impending death should not be automatically assumed without similar indications elsewhere in the hands.

Supportive evidence, such as a poor head line and heart line, or breaks in both these lines at similar points in the life, must be considered in conjunction with the state of the Mercury line and the relative strength of all these lines in both hands. So, by all means warn the subject of potential troubles and indicate the best ways of avoiding these. But, *under no circumstances advise a client of impending death*; this would be unethical, totally irresponsible and unrealistic in any case because such an event cannot be accurately dated.

Further, only a very close scrutiny (using a powerful magnifying glass) of the subject's hand prints will reveal positive indication in sufficient detail to reach a firm conclusion in such matters. For example, there may be a hairline connecting the two breaks, indicating recovery, and such a marking would not be visible to the naked eye. Alternatively, the breaks may be surrounded by a square formation which is always an indication of protection from whatever problems are threatening at the time. Again, such a formation may not always be immediately visible.

Remember, although the life line is concerned with health and the subject's approach to life, these are no more than general interpretations and all the information I have given must be only regarded as guidelines.

10

The Heart Line

The heart line can begin on the Jupiter mount, between the first and second fingers, from the extreme radial edge of the palm, or it may have a forked beginning. If forked, one line may come from between the two fingers mentioned and the other from the lower part of the mount of Jupiter. This line relates to all emotional matters, the vascular system and certain health factors.

The Start of the Line

Some palmists suggest that the heart line cannot have a beginning or an ending and others dispute which is which. Traditionally, the starting point for this line is where I have just indicated, but one modern school of thought reverses this, claiming that it commences where the traditionalists state it ends: on the mount of Mercury.

The modernists argue that all emotions are instinctive, so the logical starting place for the heart line would be on the instinctive (ulna) side of the hand. This controversy may be heightened by the fact that the heart line often forks in the Jupiter mount area, whereas the head and life lines rarely commence in a similar fashion although they frequently fork where they end.

Certainly there seems to be some justification for doubting the traditional approach in this matter because the timing of events on the heart line is particularly difficult and it would, perhaps, be easier to start at the percussion for this purpose.

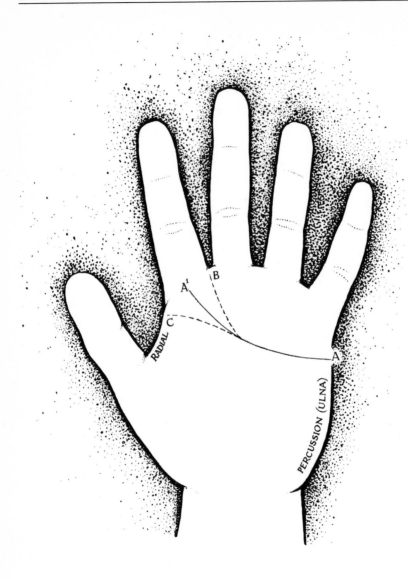

Figure 18   **VARIATIONS OF THE HEART LINE**

Key
A–A₁   The most common heart line
A–B   A practical heart line
A–C   A caring, sympathetic heart line

However, I have used the traditional method in this book although I would suggest that you investigate the alternatives.

If the heart line begins from the mount of Jupiter, curves nice and smoothly, runs under the fingers to the percussion and is clear, with no interference marks, the subject's basic emotional approach will be balanced though idealistic. The deeper this line curves into the hand, the more the emotions will be expressed physically; the shorter the curve, the more prevalent the mental side of the nature is likely to be.

A healthy balance between idealism and practicality is indicated when the heart line starts from between the first and second fingers. The closer this line is to the Saturn mount, the more practical the subject's emotional outlook; such people do not get carried away easily.

If the line commences on the Saturn mount, it denotes that the emotional side of the nature will be governed largely by sensuality, particularly if the line curves deeply. However, such people can sometimes be very cold, selfish and sexual because of their inability to understand the more sensitive needs of others.

When the line begins with a fork, with one branch coming from Jupiter and the other from Saturn, the stronger line will indicate which side of the nature dominates. An influence line extending into the lower part of the Jupiter mount denotes a caring attitude towards others. Such a subject will often make a career in nursing, teaching or social work and the likely practical application of this trait will be shown by other indications in the hand.

If a fork from this line touches the head and life lines at its beginning, it signifies a great danger. At the very least, it indicates a sudden and traumatic shock from which the subject may never really recover and which will leave its mark physically, mentally or emotionally. A triple forking at the beginning of the heart line, however, shows a well-starred and fortunate life.

General Appearance

Ideally, this line should be clear and of even colour throughout. Cross-bars and interference marks of any kind relate to emotionally stressful incidents.

A deeply etched line which is dark in colour, especially when compared to the other two main lines, is an indication of possible vascular problems, emotional hypertension or erratic forays into all kinds of relationships.

A wide space between the heart and head lines implies an extrovert and objective personality and a narrow space denotes the reverse. A long heart line signifies depth of feeling, a short line indicates coldness and a broken or chained line implies changeability.

When the heart line is noticeably longer than the head line the subjects are usually very emotional; however, in subjects where the head line is longer, their heads will literally rule their hearts.

If the heart line appears to lie straight across the top of the palm, from one edge of the hand to the other, it signifies a strong desire for affection. These people usually have such intense feelings that they cannot bear to be away from their loved ones. Of course, sheer practicality makes this impossible; as a result such subjects may give the impression of being continually unhappy.

Influences

Many fine lines dropping away from the heart line may be interpreted as signifying the sort of person who is in love with love. These folk need constant reassurance and therefore frequently change partners in their search for adulation, without which they do not thrive.

Where the line dips and touches the head line, especially under the Saturn finger, it denotes a disastrous and sometimes fateful passion, either for a person or a cause.

Influence lines dropping away from the heart line usually relate to disappointments. In particular, a branch, fork, or strong influence line dropping to the fate line may indicate the loss of a partner.

A strongly marked difference between the left and right hand heart lines should be carefully noted. The line in the left hand shows the basic pattern of the emotional make-up; the line in the right hand indicates to what extent these traits have been developed and modified to meet everyday life.

11

The Fate Line

This line bears several names: fate line, line of destiny, environment line, line of milieu, career or Saturn line. Its presence in a hand can be a restrictive factor because, although it governs ambitions, those aims are always subject to the limitations imposed by the individual's faith, or lack of it, in his or her ability. Consequently, subjects who doubt their ability to transcend their natural environment are unlikely to succeed in this aim.

Although this line is not always found in the hands of extremely successful people, in the world of sport it is often present in the hands of those who succeed in a field where precision is the prime factor: the professional racing driver, snooker or billiards player, or archer, for example.

Theoretically, the fate line runs from the wrist to the base of the Saturn finger but, in practice, it may start almost anywhere on the palm and end virtually anywhere. It can vary a great deal in length and strength, sometimes only running for a couple of centimetres or an inch or so, or perhaps appearing and reappearing at intervals. However, a clear, straight line with few or no interruptions which starts at the centre of the wrist and runs right up to the medius denotes success, individuality and the usual accompanying self-centredness.

Family Influences and the Start of the Line

The wider the gap between the fate and life lines, the less family ties have inhibited the subject's aims. Often, the career has enjoyed a relatively trouble-free start and has been realised at an early age. However, when the fate line is tied to the life line or starts inside this line, on the mount of Venus, the subject may have experienced difficulties in getting started owing to troublesome emotional ties in the early years.

A fate line that starts on the Venus mount also often implies that the subject has been expected to enter the family business or follow a career chosen by his or her parents. Occasionally, a fate line may start inside the life line but soon fade out and another line may form at about the same place or a little further up the hand. This is indicative of dutiful offspring who have followed family dictates until they have either tired of so doing or have broken free to follow their own inclinations.

When the fate line starts on the mount of Luna, success will depend largely on the approval of others and subjects with formation often enter public life or make their careers in show business or sport. An influence line entering the fate line from the Luna mount denotes an influence entering the life, but it can also indicate a career change. Influence lines that simply pass through this line have no lasting effects on the subject's career.

A late starting line, that is one that begins on the plain of Mars or from the head line, indicates that ambitions are present but there is no opportunity to put these into practice. However, such ambitions are sometimes realised eventually, particularly if the fate line starts from the head, indicating the success of long-term plans.

A clearly marked fate line starting from the heart line refers to a hobby or spare-time interest that eventually leads to a career. This can be verified by the presence of a loop in the skin pattern between the second and third fingers.

Regular and Irregular Lines

A full, long and strong fate line does not necessarily signify success or failure but it does show an awareness of duty. It may indicate a set path which the individual feels is inescapable, particularly if this line begins from the mount of Neptune. These people are fatalists at heart and their belief in this may be unshakeable.

An irregular or intermittent fate line indicates that the subject has attempted to implement many ideals, but without much actual success. Small influence lines running parallel to the fate line are indicative of minor triumphs on the path to the greater glory. Very fine influence lines running up the hand from the fate line denote successful attempts towards the desired aims whereas lines dropping away from the main line traditionally refer to failure.

In a full hand, an irregular line or intermittent line denotes a lack of tenacity to achieve the desired ambition. It is rare to find a fate line in an empty hand, but it denotes strong determination when it is present. The absence of a fate line on such a hand implies that the subject lacks a sense of direction and drive.

Terminations

When the fate line apparently stops for no reason at all, it usually indicates that severe problems have arisen with which the subject has been unable to cope. It may refer to an accident or incident which has proved too much for the subject: he or she has simply given up making the effort required.

A fate line that terminates at the head line implies a serious error of judgement by the subject, but if it stops at the heart line this denotes an emotional cause behind its ending.

A change of direction towards the Jupiter finger shows a change of direction in the ambitions or an alteration in the career. If the fate line terminates on the mount of Jupiter, it denotes success. A change of direction towards Apollo indicates an inclination towards the arts and intellectual pursuits; if the direction is towards Mercury, the trend will be towards science and industry.

Sometimes the fate line forks before it stops. In such cases, the influences denoted by both the end points should be considered. For example, if one branch of the fate line ends on the Jupiter mount and the other on the mount of Mercury, both mounts will have an effect on the aims or ambitions of the subject.

Other Marks

A square may sometimes be seen on the fate line, or between the fate and life lines, or on the percussion side of the hand. A square over a break in the fate line denotes protection from financial or business ruin. Between the fate and life lines it shows protection from danger and, if lying close to the fate line on the percussion side, it is believed to protect the subject from danger while travelling.

Cross-bars on the line show serious setbacks at the time indicated, especially if they appear heavier than the main line. Should the fate line end in a star, it denotes disgrace and a fall from favour.

An island on the line signifies a temporary weakening effect that will prevent subjects from following their chosen career. Should the fate line begin with an island, an element of mystery surrounds the subject's business connections or interest. At the end of the line, an island refers to a loss of power and prestige.

12

The Minor Lines

There are many minor lines likely to appear in any one palm and, especially in a 'full' hand, there may be some initial difficulty trying to correctly identify which line is which. Trace each line carefully and take your time – it will all fall into place with practice.

The Sun Line

The Sun line is a 'sister' line to the fate line and is frequently mistaken for a Mercury line and therefore regarded with undue reverence. Whenever it is present on the hand, it may safely be assumed that its owner is a happy person. This happiness is derived from the pleasure such people derive from their way of life, no matter what their status.

A Sun line that runs from the wrist to the Apollo finger shows a long, happy, rich life with social distinction and prestige. However, this should not be confused with the power of money and riches. These people possess inner happiness and any social distinction they earn will arise from the way in which they conduct their lives. Such subjects could just as easily be filing clerks as tycoons, but they will have that special touch which sets them apart from their fellows, thereby earning the respect and admiration of others for all they do.

If the Sun line starts inside the life line, it implies that the subject has been helped along the way in their career by the family. Less family aid and more personal achievement is indicated when this line itself starts from the life line. A Sun line rising from the mount of Luna denotes good public relations in

a career concerned with public receptivity such as enter-
tainment, literature and the arts.

A late start, based on sheer persistence, is indicated when
this line starts from the zone of Mars, whereas a forked
beginning refers to more than one career. Such people are
likely to have more than one string to their bow; they may have
a dual career or practise two entirely different professions, both
eventually bringing success.

A determination to succeed is shown when the Sun line
rises from the head line, but strong emotional overtones to the
chosen path are indicated by a heart line start. Curiously,
although a heart line start also indicates a late start to the career,
such subjects seldom want for anything in their lives.

If the line of the Sun finishes at the head line, it implies a
potential disaster in the success gained at that time; if it stops at
the heart line, emotional drawbacks to any success gained are
indicated. Possible emotional errors are also implied by this
latter formation. A Sun line that alternately fades and
reappears denotes a brilliant start to the career, but later any
success gained will be frittered away, sometimes accompanied by
poor attempts to recoup the loss.

An influence line that starts from the heart line and cuts
into the Sun line indicates a troublesome period or, according
to traditional palmistry, an active enemy or rival. A similar line
starting from the head line and cutting into the line of the Sun
indicates miscalculations that result in losses, mainly financial
ones.

When the fate and Sun lines merge, it denotes that the
owner will realise all his or her ambitions. A branch line from
the fate line to the Sun line has a similar meaning although, in
this case, it implies benefits received through the assistance of
someone close. But a marriage line from the mount of Mercury
which cuts into the Sun line and then stops indicates an
emotional entanglement ending in disgrace.

The Mercury Line

One hopes that this line will not be present on the hand; but if
it is, it refers to a lasting health problem or weakness, possibly a

recurring illness or even a mild form of hypochondria.

When this line runs from the life line to the mount of Mercury, the subject will be very aware of health matters. Such people may be diet- or hygiene-conscious, avoid certain proprietary drugs or perhaps insist on taking daily vitamin capsules. However, if the Mercury line does not touch the life line, there is no reason why the subject should not enjoy a long and healthy life, within the limits already mentioned.

But a Mercury line that starts from the mount of Venus denotes a weakness in the digestive system and if this line twists, frays or is wavy, the subject rarely enjoys good health. The usual weakness is biliousness, poor digestion or, if the subject has a full hand which denotes a 'natural worrier', even ulcers.

Sometimes the Mercury line forms a distinct cross with the head line, indicating a possible interest in occult matters and, if these lines combine with the fate line to form a distinct triangle, the subject usually has an aptitude for the occult sciences. Such people are naturally intuitive, play their hunches and can easily be trained as psychic healers.

The Line of Intuition

This small, semicircular line begins on the mount of Luna, curves into the centre of the palm and ends on the Mercury mount; it denotes a natural intuition which is frequently used by its owner.

Invariably, such people automatically gravitate to occult matters. They possess an investigative nature and retentive memory, have read widely and can express themselves fluently. These subjects have an uncanny gift for 'knowing' what will happen and this will be accentuated if the Neptune mount is well-developed.

If a line of intuition appears on an elementary hand, it implies that the subject is at one with nature.

The Girdle of Venus

This girdle is normally formed by a series of small broken lines curving across the mounts between the heart line and the base of the fingers. It implies emotional hypersensitivity and intensifies aesthetic appreciation.

But this sensitivity occasionally appears on the physical level as a form of irritability or restlessness. Such subjects crave activity and excitement and will go to extreme lengths to satisfy their appetites; cross-bars which cut through the girdle will emphasize this trait.

The Via Lasciva

The Via Lasciva, or allergy line, often takes the form of one well-marked line that crosses the base of the mount of Luna towards the mount of Venus. However, if this line is broken, chained or islanded, it does not refer to an allergy. If composed of very fine lines, it denotes a physical need for stimulants such as drugs, drink or sex. If a girdle is also present on the hand, this tendency will be accentuated.

Subjects with both these markings in the hand will need to exercise control if they are not to succumb to these tendencies. Unfortunately, they always give way to their senses and passions at one time or another. But a good head line will denote the control necessary to counteract these tendencies.

The Ring of Solomon

This marking is a small line that curves round the base of the Jupiter finger. Traditionally, it confers wisdom, bestows the power of authority and the ability to teach and inclines the owner towards philosophical studies.

The Ring of Saturn

Again, this is a small line encircling the base of a finger: the Saturn, or middle, finger. It implies an imbalance in the subject's psychological make-up because the balancing effect of the Saturn finger is 'cut off' from the palm.

The Rascettes

The rascettes, or bracelets, are the lines that run across the inside of the wrist, at the base of the palm. Usually there are one, two or three of these lines present, but there may be more. Eastern palmistry credits them with more significance than does the Western school of thought. Traditionally, these lines were linked with longevity, but in practice this does not seem to be the case.

If the first line arches into the base of the palm on a woman's hand, it is a strong indication of difficulties in the genito-urinary system: anything from bladder to menstrual problems.

It is therefore particularly worth noting in the hands of young girls, as problems will sometimes arise which can be easily alleviated by correct treatment, thus saving embarrassment in adolescence and avoiding any future health problems of this nature.

If the second rascette also arches upward, the difficulties described above will be aggravated. In such circumstance, any third line present is likely to be chained or weak-looking. When the rascettes simply traverse the wrist in a normal manner, these particular problems should not arise. However, should the reproductive system be upset, in the event of a hysterectomy for instance, this is sometimes reflected in the top rascette which may begin to arch upwards.

The bracelets are also concerned with travel matters. Fine lines rising vertically from the rascettes into the mount of Luna denote long journeys and, the more numerous the lines, the more travel is indicated. Once again, read the travel lines in the normal way: if these rising lines are not present, the subject is not likely to travel much.

The Family Ring

This is the name given to the chained formation which runs around the base of the second phalange of the thumb, separating it from the mount of Venus. If it is heavy and well-marked, it denotes considerable family ties throughout the life; but when there are few or no family links this line will almost completely fade out.

Influence lines usually traverse the Venus mount from this ring towards the life line. If these influence lines end at, or short of, the life line, they refer to private family matters that have left a lasting impression on the subject. However, if these lines travel beyond the life line, their termination will indicate the likely effects of the family's influence.

For example, a line which stops at the fate line and significantly alters its appearance beyond the terminal point implies that family matters have caused an alteration in the subject's chosen path at that time.

Marriage and Children Lines

These are the small horizontal and vertical lines on the percussion side of the mount of Mercury, just above the heart line. Traditionally, the horizontal lines denote marriage and the vertical lines indicate children, but I prefer to read horizontal lines as referring to a place or home where the subject may safely rest, whether this is the home of parents, in-laws or a close friend. The vertical lines can be interpreted as referring to those people who occupy or belong in that place.

Medical Stigmata

Sometimes, there are three or four short vertical lines slightly to one side of the Mercury finger, just above the heart line known as the medical stigmata and signifying an aptitude for healing. This formation indicate a nursing career, veterinary work or any calling concerned with helping people.

Occasionally, the medical stigmata are confused with similar marks which refer to dental problems but, if neither explanation is applicable, it can indicate slight hypochondria.

Travel Lines

Travel indications are found in several places in the palm. One specific traditional location for travel lines is on the mount of Luna. A number of fine lines may enter the palm from the percussion side of the hand, below the level of the head line.

If straight, with no interference or breaks, each line denotes a long-desired journey safely completed. If the line turns upwards at its end, it shows a successful conclusion to the adventure; if it turns downwards, unsuccessful; and if it ends in a cross, it implies a disappointment.

A square on the line protects the subject from dangers, and the journey undertaken may be a brilliant success if this line terminates with a star. An islanded line denotes an unsatisfactory conclusion. A circle on the line, especially at its end, may indicate danger from drowning.

13

Special Marks

A wide variety of 'special marks' may be found in a hand, and in almost any position. The marks mentioned here are those referred to in Western palmistry but the indications traditionally used in Hindu palmistry have not been included.

The Dot

The dot is a mark frequently found on lines. It indicates an obstruction whose effects may be greater or less according to its appearance.

A heavy dot on a light line signifies a temporary loss of the effect of that line whereas a light dot on a heavy line may not have any effect at all. A series of dots close together may refer to a recurring problem that gives the subject difficulty for as long as this mark continues to be seen.

When two major lines meet with a dot exactly on the junction, it usually refers to a delaying factor. This will be of a temporary nature and its effect will vary according to the lines involved.

The Square

This formation is always a sign of protection, no matter whereabouts on the hand it is located. If it should surround a break in a line, it always implies that whatever the individual circumstances may be the owner will bring a problem to a successful conclusion and will win through to success and happiness in the end.

The Circle

A circle occurs only rarely and can be a good influence or bad, depending on its position. Often the circle formation is slightly misshapen and accidentally identified as an island.

The circle is most commonly seen on the heart line and refers to eye trouble or weakness if located below the Apollo finger, or deafness if located below the Saturn finger. A small, clear circle on the thumb side of the life line may also refer to sight problems and, traditionally, a half-circle means only one eye will be involved.

On the Apollo mount, a circle signifies brilliance if it is found next to the end of the Sun line. On the mount of the Moon, this formation refers to danger involving water. My own experience has proved this to be true: I have seen this mark twice on the mount of the Moon and in both cases the owner was drowned in tragic circumstances.

Grilles

Grilles represent a destructive force, no matter where they occur, because they diminish energy and fritter away any good which may be there. They are most common on the full hand, where there is invariably a grille formation to be seen on the Venus mount and this signifies that the subject's physical energies are being wasted in pointless activities.

When located on a mount, the grille formation takes away most of the relevant good qualities, and when on a line it seriously impedes the power of that line. It may even add to the poor qualities displayed in a poor hand.

Triangles

Triangles usually indicate intellectual talent or creative abilities wherever they are located. Such a marking must be a distinct and separate formation away from random lines and be clearly recognisable as such.

On the mount of Jupiter, for example, a triangle signifies the subject's strength of diplomacy and tact; on the Apollo mount it may indicate an architectural talent, although this is largely a traditional view.

The Cross

Whether found as an individual mark or formed by minor influence lines crossing other lines, the cross usually signifies an unfavourable time. On a line, a cross interferes with the qualities signified by this line; on its own, it weakens the effect denoted by its site, especially if clearly located on a mount.

Some of the traditional interpretations of the cross formation are a little hard to accept. For example, it is considered to be a fortunate sign to have a cross between the mount of the Moon and the quadrangle, implying safety at sea.

Bars

A bar signifies a hindrance stronger than a dot. If deeply etched and isolated from other chance markings, it denotes a temporary struggle. Where a line appears weaker after the bar, it implies that whatever this difficulty was, it has left its mark.

The Star

This formation is considered to intensify the effects of the location on which it is found. It is a good sign unless it is on, or at the end of, a line, where it can presage serious trouble.

In the middle of a line, the star refers to a serious illness or accident occurring at that time. What is more, anyone with such a mark may never fully recover from the incident or setback.

On the head line, the star denotes mental or head problems; on the life line, it signifies injury; and on the heart line, it may refer to an emotional shock or heart attack.

When placed at the end of the line of destiny or the Sun line, it implies great personal success, although this carries the chance of disaster. Such people walk a tightrope between fame and notoriety, the distance between the two being minimal;

and, if they are public favourites, the world almost waits for them to put a foot wrong, as they invariably do.

Islands

Islands always have a weakening effect. Any line with an island in it cannot perform its function properly until the islanding has finished; there are no exceptions.

The Trident

The trident is mostly associated with Eastern palmistry, but it appears to have been adopted by the West. It is rarely seen, and then only in conjunction with lines. It is believed to confer brilliance and success, relevant to its location.

For example, a major line that ended in a distinct, three-pronged fork, such as the fate line or Sun line, would indicate a threefold success at whatever was attempted. Such an achievement would, of course, bring the subject appropriate recognition.

Tassels, Chains and Breaks

These three marks all indicate a lessening of natural energies. For example, a tassel at the end of a line indicates a weakening of the abilities associated with that line with the onset of old age. A break has more serious implications as it signifies a break in the continuity of the power denoted by the line on which it appears. However, only a print of the hands will confirm the existence of a distinct break. If sited on both hands, a break implies that serious health problems may arise, particularly when the life, head and heart lines are involved.

A chain formation always denotes weakness and a continuously chained line indicates a continuing weakness. In the case of the life line, for example, the health or constitution will always be weak, probably with a recurring illness. There is no reason, however, why the subject may not live a long and happy life, although it will be within the context of the health factor involved.

The Quadrangle

The area of the palm which lies between the heart and head lines is known as the quadrangle. Ideally, except for the fate and Sun lines crossing this area, it should be clear of all other influence marks.

Sometimes the heart and head lines run almost parallel and the quadrangle thus formed will present an even appearance, denoting a well-balanced personality. However, the

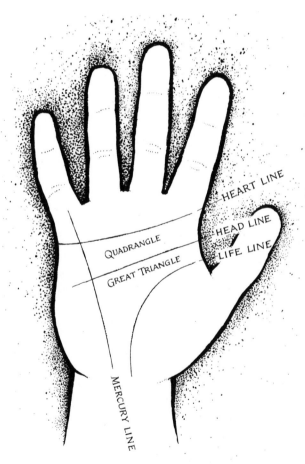

Figure 19
THE QUADRANGLE AND THE GREAT TRIANGLE

more the heart line dips towards the head line, the more the emotional side of the nature will dominate; if the head line rises towards the heart line, the subject is likely to be more practical and self-reliant.

The Great Triangle

The great triangle is the area enclosed by the life, head and Mercury lines. Like the quadrangle, it should be fairly clear of influence lines, well-defined and quite long. Sometimes the hand lacks a Mercury line but a line of intuition is present; in such a case the subject is likely to be psychically gifted and very fortunate.

A wide angle between the head and life lines indicates an impetuous nature; a narrow angle denotes caution; and a triangle which looks well-balanced on the hand implies a good sense of drama and dramatic talent. Often, public figures have this latter configuration which, with a good Luna mount, adds a little extra 'zing' to the personality.

The Mystic Cross

This is a clearly-defined mark which is found in the quadrangle (no part of the cross may be formed by any major or minor influence lines). It indicates an interest in the occult, spiritualism, healing or other philosophies associated with the hidden sciences and arts.

If this cross is located below the Saturn finger, the owner is less likely to practise such philosophies but will be more inclined to study them. However, if sited below the Apollo, the subject is more likely to practise than study these arts. In either case, the presence of the mystic cross implies that such subjects will have the natural gifts necessary to fulfil their desires.

The Life-saving Cross

This formation may be found between the fate line and the life line, about 2 cm/1 in above the wrist. It does not necessarily mean that the subjects will actually save life but that they may be presented with the opportunity to do so in the course of their lives, either professionally or by chance. Such a person may, for example, be an ambulance driver or serve on a life-boat; or be one of those people who are so compassionate and humanitarian that others instinctively turn to them when in need of help and advice.

White Lines

Small horizontal lines are sometimes seen along the top phalanges of the palmar side of the fingertips. The length of these lines can vary considerably from a couple of centimetres to the whole width of the finger. On hand prints they show up as simple white lines, hence their name. They can be seen very clearly on the fingertips of a full hand (see fig 10 on page 60).

Whenever found, they imply a general weakening of the health. Such subjects may, for instance, have been burning the candle at both ends and is probably living on nervous energy, having depleted their natural physical resources.

With adequate rest and sensible diet, these lines fade as the subject's natural stamina returns. But, if bad habits continue, the weakest point in the health will be the first to collapse under any strain, and it may take some time to repair the damage.

14

Dating Systems

The measurement of time is one of the most difficult aspects of the study of palmistry. Establishing time can be a complex business because there are no universally accepted hard and fast rules. In fact, several differing schools of thought exist in this rather grey area.

However, it is generally accepted that the life line is the easiest to start with, followed by the fate and Sun lines. These last two should be read together because they are so often inextricably linked, assuming, of course, that they both appear on the hand. The head line should be considered next, although there may be a problem here in the event of a short line, and the heart line and bracelets should be ignored.

An imaginary line drawn vertically down the palm from the centre of the base of the index finger will intersect the life line at a point representing the age of 10 approximately. A second line, taken from the middle of the gap between the index and medius fingers, will cut into the life line at age 20; and age 35, approximately, will be shown by a line drawn directly to the life line from the centre of the base of the middle finger.

So, the beginning of the life line to the first intersection represents roughly 10 years and, if you divide this length in two, you get the five-year mark. Divide the 10- and 20-year marks by two to give the 15-year mark and, continuing in this way, divide the space between the 20- and 35-year marks to find the 27/28-year point. Assuming that life expectancy is 70, dividing the end of the life line and the 35-year mark by two will indicate the 52/53–year point, and so on.

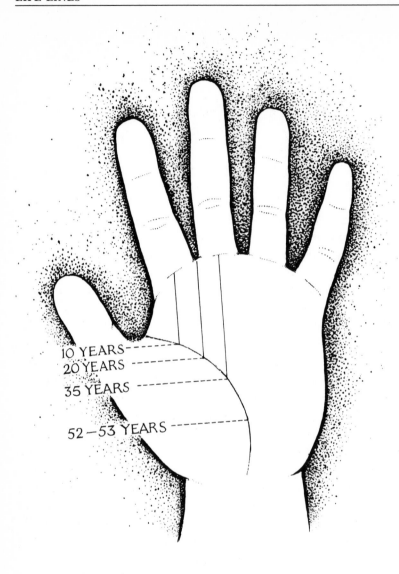

Figure 20

DATING SYSTEM USING THE LINE OF LIFE

Obviously, after the 35-year mark, the dating of events is likely to become a problem because of the difference between life lines on each hand. Certainly, the first part of this dating system is more accurate than the last but, once you have verified a few dates with your subject, the rest should fall into place without too much trouble and confirmation of the later time-scale can be found by the dating method for the fate line.

If the fate line is long or ends on the Saturn mount, the point where it intersects the head line is approximately at the age of 35 and where it cuts the heart line is roughly 45. Take the area from the base of the palm to the head line, and divide this into three sections, so that each of these sections of the fate line will represent roughly 10 to 12 years. An allowance of 25 years should be made for the section between the heart line and the mount of Saturn.

The same dating method can be used for the Sun line except that the measurements will be to the Apollo mount (the termination of the Sun line).

Sometimes there is no fate line on the hand but, when there is, dating events on the head line is made much easier. The first half of the head line represents birth to 35 years old and the second half from 35 to 70 approximately. Again, each section of the head line can be divided into halves, then divided again and again in order to date events.

This basically simple technique will, with a little practice, enable you to date events with reasonable accuracy. However, when in consultation with a subject, the occasional simple question should soon establish the time pattern on the hand you are examining. There is no harm in asking if an event occurred at a specific time and, if the answer is 'yes', using that point as the basis for all timing.

It is simply not possible to date events accurately to a day, month or year. If numerology or astrology are used in conjunction with chirology, then a specific date may possibly be found, but not when palmistry alone is being practised, because no completely satisfactory method of dating has yet been devised.

The palmistry system used in the East is complex and alien to Western thinking although it is, up to a point, very accurate.

However, a student would need to practise much Eastern palmistry in order to understand fully the timing system used and this is, unfortunately, beyond the scope of this book.

Research groups in this country have recently come to regard even the fate line system outlined in this chapter with some suspicion. Accurate dating certainly is the weakest point of modern palmistry, but probably it is also the most fascinating.

Another problem which can arise relates to health matters. Certain areas of the palm are specifically concerned with signs of ill health and, in such cases, the time factor must be ignored completely.

So, the safest and most reliable dating method is to look at the life lines, and it is in this area that you should concentrate your best efforts.

15

Dermatoglyphics: The Fingers

The skin pattern is composed of tiny capillary lines and furrows across the entire surface of the palm, from the very edges of the hand to the tips of the fingers. History and experience have taught us that these patterns never change. Every attempt to erase, alter or transpose them has proved useless: they cannot be destroyed.

The skin pattern will be seen to break up during illness or health variations brought about by diet deficiency, emotional worry affecting the physical well-being, or mental illness. But, once the subject is back on the path to recovery, the pattern will resume a healthy appearance again.

Personality traits associated with skin patterns are considered to refer to the basic character make-up and are known to be of an hereditary nature. They tend to represent the unchangeable and fundamental background to the way we interpret life and, as they never alter, it is easy to see how they become associated with chirological interpretation. The advances made over the last 30 or 40 years in this particular area of study have been systematically and methodically undertaken not only by students of palmistry, but by hospital staff, university units and other research groups involved in the better understanding of human beings, medically, psychologically and chirologically.

There are five basic patterns that appear on the fingers and thumbs although there are variations in each of the patterns. The basic patterns are the whorl, arch, tented arch, loop and composite.

WHORL ULNA LOOP RADIAL LOOP

Figure 21 **FINGER PATTERNS**

The Whorl

No matter where it is found, the basic characteristic displayed by this pattern is one of individualism and originality. Self-assurance, obstinacy and a large degree of ambition are usually inherent in such a personality. Some degree of loneliness may be present in subjects with this fingerprint pattern and they can be very difficult to influence, especially once they have made up their minds about something. Such subjects possess purpose, zeal and enthusiasm, and often take up research and experimental work.

The Loop

Open-mindedness and warmth of character are the underlying characteristics of subjects with this skin pattern. They frequently take the least line of resistance because of their preference for peace and quiet, though not at any cost. An inherent flexibility of approach is displayed by these subjects who are versatile and adaptable. They express themselves easily and lean towards the arts rather than the sciences but, if emotionally disturbed, fly from one extreme to the other very quickly.

ARCH   TENTED ARCH

Figure 22   **FINGER PATTERNS**

The Arch

This pattern indicates a certain guardedness of approach and a somewhat repressed emotional outlook. Such subjects take life seriously, often with a grim determination, but lack subtlety and rarely fulfil their ambitions because they may not always be certain of these in the first place. They do not give in easily and can be intractable and a little suspicious of the motives of others.

The Tented Arch

Extreme sensitivity, an artistic nature and impulsiveness are the keywords for this pattern. Constantly aspiring to greater things, idealistic and often musically inclined, these subjects display great enthusiasm when a new subject or object takes their fancy. Unfortunately, the complete make-up may lack proper balance because these people tend to lack good judgement when it is most needed.

COMPOSITE   COMPOUND

Figure 23   **FINGER PATTERNS**

The Composite

This pattern looks like entwined loops and indicates a mind that is always open to opposing views and impressions. It is rare for such subjects to accept anything without fully exploring all the possibilities involved because they like to look at the contrasting elements of anything and everything that affects them. Unbending and sometimes stubborn beyond belief, they are very down to earth and can show surprising practical ability when they so choose.

The Compound

There are more groups or patterns, which are for the most part variations on those above, but the last I shall mention is the compound. This is usually a mixture of the loop and the whorl, although it could be composed of an arch and loop, or any other two patterns. If the pattern is definitely not of the twin loop variety, or composite, it should be read as a compound of whichever patterns are involved and the interpretation adjusted to the patterns incorporated.

Positioning of the Patterns

The relative positions of the various fingerprint patterns are important to note as these indicate which areas of the subjects' make-up dominate and influence their actions and interpretation of the patterns should be adjusted accordingly. The higher the pattern is located on the finger, the more the ideals and abstract and mental approaches of the subject are utilised; the lower the position, the more their practical nature is employed. Midway positions are, therefore, the most beneficial because a fine balance between the practical and the idealistic side of the character can be struck.

Equally important is the individual finger or thumb on which these patterns appear. Each digit has a specific 'characteristic' and these, too, should be taken into consideration when interpreting the skin patterns.

The Whorl

When found on the index finger, this pattern indicates an intensification of the subject's ambitions which may often be original or unique. Such people tend to be rather unadaptable, are usually very self-determined, make up their minds early in life and rarely depart from the set path. They make good leaders although they tend to fight shy of the limelight if they can. You should never tell these subjects what to do or order them about: you have to ask them politely.

The whorl pattern on the middle finger shows that the subject has an analytical nature which will be utilised either professionally or as a hobby. Strongly self-exploratory, such people usually hold highly individual opinions and like to find out everything for themselves. They are not easily swayed by the opinions of others and exhibit strong feelings of self-protection and determination.

On the third finger, the whorl pattern indicates people who are positive and often unconventional in their attitude towards fashion and art. They learn through experience and keep their emotions on a tight rein; their feelings are based on defined patterns and they are rarely, if ever, shaken from these.

A little finger with whorls shows an individual who is not easily influenced by what he or she sees or hears. Such people carefully select only those things that really interest them, discard the rest and, given the opportunity, can talk the hind leg off a donkey.

It is rare indeed to find a whorl on a 'weak' thumb because this pattern indicates that will-power is brought to bear slowly and that, although the ensuing actions may be equally slow, they will be virtually unstoppable. Stubborn, but persevering, these subjects eventually achieve their aims and, if this pattern occurs on both thumbs, it indicates the true individualist.

The Loop

A loop on the index finger denotes versatility in ambitious and spiritual concepts. These subjects have a graceful, charming manner and adapt to new ideas and plans and participate well in most spheres. If in positions of leadership, they attain respect through their thoughtfulness.

If found on the middle finger, the loop indicates people who tend not to hold long-term opinions about anything. Adaptable, frank and open, they dislike bias in others. Philosophy often attracts them because it allows the mind to remain open to all sorts of theories and concepts which can be continually mulled over but will not necessarily be adhered to.

A third finger loop indicates artistic and emotional appreciation and freedom. Usually inhibited, these folk quickly climb on the bandwagon of new fads and fashions, find it easy to display self-expression, but are emotionally orientated.

The little finger loop denotes there is an easy assimilation of new ideas. Perceptive and impulsive, these subjects exhibit an easy manner and have a tendency to be able to say and do the right thing at the right time although they usually find it easier to be verbally fluent than to express themselves in other ways.

On the thumb, a loop shows a deftness and flexibility of purpose. Although basically impulsive, these subjects can display skill and dexterity if they find themselves in difficult situations as a result of their impulsive actions. Their well-practised art of diplomacy comes into play when their tendency to go where angels fear to tread backfires.

The Arch

An arch pattern on the index finger shows a realistic streak: the personality will be intense and persevering. These subjects may often change the direction of their beliefs and actions, even after they have held to a set of self-imposed rules for a long time. They impress others with a sense of power rather than charm.

On the middle finger, the arch pattern indicates the subject's tendency to avoid the discussion of personal aims and beliefs. Such people lack a clear-cut direction but do not like to admit this. Their self-expression is often rather inhibited, sometimes leading to a slight lack of balance.

A third finger arch is a rare occurrence, but when found, denotes a lack of abstract artistic expression. These subjects do, however, possess a strong practical streak and may well find beauty in construction rather than in nature: bridges, ships, even lorries and trains can appeal to these people.

On the fourth finger, the arch indicates the subject's practical expertise in areas of self-preservation. Verbal fluency is often lacking and these people may have difficulty in grasping new ideas although they make money – but only enough to live comfortably.

On the thumb, the arch pattern is a mark of self-preservation, brought about by suspicion of the motives of others. Such subjects may appear to be rather intense, yet they usually possess efficiency in practical matters and have a good, sound common-sense approach to life.

The Tented Arch

This pattern denotes the enthusiasts of life: the ever-young, the intense reformer who wants to set the world to rights by teatime. This pattern is at its most expressive when it appears on the index finger because these subjects will always try to live up to their maximum potential at all times.

On the medius, the tented arch indicates a tendency to be too idealistic. Such subjects can become so caught up by their philosophies that they forget to take time off to study the practical effects of their interests – to the detriment of their day-to-day existence.

When found on the third finger, one can expect an emotionally highly-strung personality: impulsive and enthusiastic, with many ideals but few of a practical nature. Artistic and musical ability are usually well-pronounced in such folk who possess an instinctive flair for dress and appearance.

It is rare to find this pattern on the fourth finger but, when it does occur, it denotes a good command of language, written and verbal. Such subjects might be expected to adapt the techniques of learning to their own unique style and are often to be found working for charitable bodies.

On the thumb, this pattern indicates a flexible approach, enabling the subject to work with all kinds of people. Will-power may be slight, but this will be more than compensated for by a charming manner and diplomatic persuasiveness.

Tented arches are very rare, however, and my remarks relating to this pattern occurring on the little finger or thumb should be taken as conjecture as no clear-cut findings are yet available.

The Composite

On the index finger, this pattern shows a conflict between ideals and concepts. Ambitions may be somewhat limited and these subjects often display poor adaptability when things go wrong. They are not very versatile except, perhaps, in the purely physical context.

A medius composite implies a rather matter-of-fact attitude towards life; philosophy of any kind rarely attracts such people. These individuals have their feet planted on the ground, and there they will stay.

A slow or restrained attitude towards artistic appreciation may be found when the composite is on the third finger. Tastes may be severe or even utilitarian and such subjects will frown on unnecessary frills and fripperies unless profit can result from incorporating art or beauty in their careers.

On the fourth finger, this pattern denotes a lack of coherent thought in business and commercial matters. Self-expression will lack fluency and it would be rare to see such subjects in influential positions in the business world.

A composite on the thumb indicates uncertainty. These people will display a slow persevering approach to all matters, particularly those of a practical nature.

16

Dermatoglyphics:
The Palmar Patterns

T he interpretation of the palmar patterns requires skill which only comes with experience and good tutoring. It can be difficult to analyse the exact nature of a pattern, its value in the overall assessment and how much it contributes to the personality make-up.

One difficulty that may arise is that a pattern can be difficult to recognise at first, or it may be only partially present or, indeed, complete absent from the hands. So, the first thing to note is the general appearance of the skin pattern. It may be tiny, with a very fine 'closed' look, or it can consist of furrows and ridges which are wide and bold in appearance compared to the rest of the hand.

A finely-textured appearance implies a naturally refined and gentle subject whose sensitivity should be apparent. Even if the rest of the indications on the hand refer to earthier traits, such as sensuality, then these would still be expressed but in a refined or sensitive way. The individual's approach is likely to be mainly a mental one: every action and reaction stems from a calculating mind. Any indication of brute force and ignorance on the part of the subject would be a façade because the mental side of the nature is always dominant.

When the overall texture of the pattern is 'open' and appears coarse, the subject's reactions are likely to be of a more physical type: the material side of the nature will predominate.

Care should be taken, however, not to be misled between texture and the actual physical quality of the hand. Firmness denotes strong, physical activity: such people like to be on the go all the time and are rarely lazy. But, should the hand feel flabby, it invariably indicates physical laziness. Such people dislike real effort, lack direction and may tend to be selfish.

Although palmar patterns vary a great deal, it is unusual to find more than a few on any individual hand. It is also important to remember that their implications must always be taken in the context of other indications in the hand. For example, just because the palmar patterns indicate musical talent or appreciation, it does not follow that the subject will appreciate Beethoven and Brahms; it might well be that they express their love of harmony by listening to or playing Country and Western music.

Loops

A loop in the palmar pattern between the base of the first and second fingers denotes qualities of leadership. It indicates strong personal magnetism and may refer to good executive ability if found on one hand only. Such a formation will certainly indicate that leadership of some kind will feature in the subject's life if it is found on both hands and, in traditional Indian palmistry, it is known as 'the Rajah', implying royal blood.

A loop may enter the palm on one hand only between the second and third fingers. This shows a strong, serious purpose somewhere in the subject's life: it may only be a hobby, or it could be an interest which will affect his or her lifestyle. If this formation appears on both hands, it often indicates a very strong interest which the subject would like to make a career of but, for some outside reason, is unable to do. This loop denotes the subject's dedication to a cause close to his or her heart, possibly one of benefit to others.

A small loop between the fourth and third fingers indicates a sense of humour, but a large loop swerving in under the third finger usually means that these subjects will display a touchy or vain streak if humour is directed against them: they may criticise themselves but cannot stand criticism from others. If the small loop is present on both hands, the subject usually possesses a

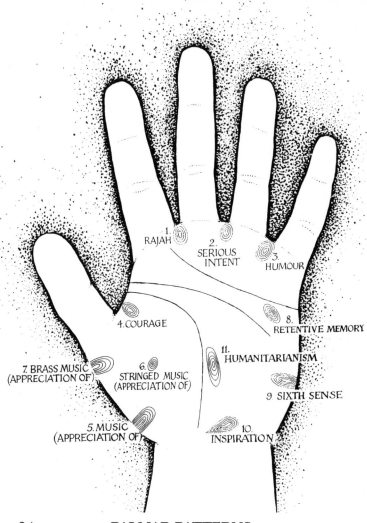

Figure 24   **PALMAR PATTERNS**

Key:

1 Rajah
2 Serious intent
3 Humour
4 Courage
5 Music (appreciation of)
6 Stringed music (appreciation of)

7 Brass music (appreciation of)
8 Retentive memory
9 Sixth sense
10 Inspiration
11 Humanitarianism

sense of the ridiculous, whereas the larger loop on both hands normally indicates a complete lack of humour.

A loop may enter the palmar pattern between the thumb and first finger, at the top of the mount of Mars. This formation denotes courage, someone who either admires acts of bravery or, indeed, may be heroic in practice, should the need arise.

Another version of this loop may be found in a similar position, although not identical, where it follows, touches or intermingles with the family ring. This position indicates the subject's persistent uphill fight to maintain family or honour.

There are three kinds of pattern which may appear lower down on the mount of Venus and each of these tends to reveal a talent or admiration for a different kind of music. If all three patterns are present on the hand, it shows a definite musical ability in the practical sense.

A long loop coming into the base of the mount from the wrist will invariably denote musical appreciation although not necessarily musical ability. People with this particular formation will find that music exerts a tremendous influence on them, even if they cannot play an instrument or compose music themselves. Sometimes, a tiny loop is formed within the patterns and lines in the middle of the mount of Venus. This indicates a preference for stringed instruments and one may safely assume that the subject prefers orchestral music to military music, brass bands and the like. A preference for the latter type of music is shown by a loop entering the pattern from the angle of time.

An elongated loop that seems to 'swim' with the patterns between the heart and head lines usually denotes a retentive memory or an ability for total recall. If the head line actually dips into this pattern, this ability will be strongly enhanced and the further this loop reaches towards the top of the Luna mount, the more efficient the memory.

If this formation appears on the left hand only, it usually means that past events will be easily recalled; however, on the right hand only, it indicates that memory will be used to facilitate career or business affairs.

A loop coming into the side of the hand from the top of the Luna mount frequently shows that nature plays a large part in the subject's life. He or she may have 'green fingers', dowsing ability or, at the very least, a 'sixth sense' which manifests itself at just the right moments in time.

Sometimes, a loop is seen to start from the base of the hand where the mount of Neptune should be. Whether the mount is developed or not, this loop almost invariably indicates strong intuition and imagination. It is a rare formation but, when it does occur, its owner seems to have an uncanny knack for doing the right thing at the right time and inspiration will usually come to the rescue when all else fails.

A less common palmar pattern occurs where a loop lies along the line of life, or the life line appears to go through the loop. The owners of such a formation are in tune with people of all kinds. They are sympathetic and have the ability to get on with others whatever the circumstances.

One other marking which may occur is a whorled effect on the mount of Luna. This shows an individualistic approach to identity; for example, actors or actresses who can totally submerge themselves into a role with complete authority. Such people can be totally ingratiating when they want something, but this manner will not be over-obvious.

This whorl can appear either as a composite or as one of the arch formations. If it appears as a composite, the subjects may be conscious that they have a gift but be unaware of the nature of their ability, or be unable to put it into practice. A tented arch shows enthusiasm for getting along with others while the ordinary arch, unless it is a definite pattern, denotes the opposite.

There has been much research into the significance of skin patterns in recent years, and such studies are still being carried out. The findings have been of great help to those who study hands in their psychiatric work. Knowledge of how to combine the gifts shown by the various skin patterns with the other attributes in the hands has proved valuable in many cases and, as these studies progress, perhaps we shall discover more useful information.

Do remember, however, that these patterns require expert interpretation and you should, therefore, take care in your assessment. This aspect of chirology is still very much in its infancy and you should be very proficient in accepted hand interpretation before delving into this complex area. If you feel at all uncertain, leave this particular aspect alone or, at the very least, seek expert guidance before you begin your assessment.

17

Gesture

It is said that people show their true nature in three ways: by their actions, words and gestures. A science within a science, the study of gesture provides an inexhaustible source of information which can help a chirologist to define certain character traits within the personality.

One aspect of hand gesture is handwriting, which is the observable result of consistent gestures shaped by intelligence. Handwriting is governed by the thoughts and actions of the individual at the time of writing and is one of the few natural gestures that cannot be completely altered by an attempt at disguise. I would recommend students of chirology to supplement their knowledge with a brief study of graphology.

Gesture is either rhythmic or unrhythmic, either smooth and flowing or awkward and gawky. Some people are ill at ease with fresh faces, whether in their social or working environment, and this will be revealed by a certain amount of restriction in their hand movements while the new personality is summed up. As the association continues and decisions are reached regarding acceptance or non-acceptance, hand gestures become more natural and less defensive.

Handshakes

Usually the first meeting between two people is marked by a handshake or nod of the head. If one person refuses to shake hands, this is not necessarily a refusal of acceptance; it usually indicates a closed personality, someone who is guarded and unsure. But a meeting that is marked by a handshake will provide you with a variety of points to observe.

Immediately before the handshake, no matter what the circumstances, both parties will have briefly summed up the other with their eyes and made subconscious decisions. The more positive of the two will advance confidently and thrust out his or her hand, the thumb slightly extended, for the other to take. This person is taking the initiative, assuming the more dominant role, for the other person has little choice but to accept the hand offered.

The grasp should be firm, last a couple of seconds, then the hands should be disengaged. Inevitably, the more dominant personality of the two will stand firm, the other will unconsciously retreat a step, having accepted the submissive role. In a business meeting this is a very important point and an observer will note that throughout the whole affair these dominant/submissive attitudes will not alter.

A powerhouse handshake is frequently met, and never forgotten. Your hand is taken, squeezed, pumped and thrown back at you. Yet such a handshake indicates a basic emotional insecurity. These individuals may appear calm and positive on the surface but are often a seething mass of emotion underneath. This imbalance may show itself as a 'hard' nature which belies the underlying constant need for self-assertion.

The anti-social handshake is equally memorable and shows a lack of character development. You are given one, two or three fingers to hold, there is minimum pressure and the grip feels like a wet fish. Your instinctive reaction is one of discomfort and guardedness, without quite knowing why. Such a handshake reveals a general disdain for people and can be offered by those who are either somewhat weak or very calculating.

There is a provocative style of handshake that often instills a sense of superiority in the recipient. With this type, you are offered a hand curled up in a ball or held so loosely that it is difficult to hold: the hand does not move of its own accord, you have to shake it. Insincerity and a marked level of emotional instability are indicated by such a handshake.

The reverse of this is the stimulating handshake: two hands

grasp your one, squeeze, pummel and shake it. Your hand will be held for just a little too long, making you feel slightly uncomfortable. Such folk may even move one of their hands to your arm, elbow or shoulder and stand a little too close, invading your personal space. These are the really emotional individuals who want to win you over to their way of thinking: they need to be your friend and want to be liked, even loved.

Interviews

If you wish to establish a rapport between yourself and a client during the course of a hand-reading session, try not to sit behind a desk while you are talking because this will destroy the personal approach completely. Remember, your clients are there seeking guidance and help and you should display warmth and compassion as they are quite likely to bare their souls to you. Sit with your client, either in separate armchairs or together on a small settee, ensure a small table is at hand for the paperwork and try to convey a relaxed but attentive manner.

In business matters, however, the desk may be used to create a superior/inferior attitude, and frequently is. In recruitment it can be an inhibiting factor, but it may also be used to determine how much confidence the interviewee possesses.

Potential recruits may sit opposite the interviewer with arms and legs crossed. This indicates defensiveness: try to get them to open up by discussing their personal interests. People's hands will come alive with gestures as they launch into their favourite subject: themselves.

People who sit with legs uncrossed and hands held loosely or just touching are showing confidence; they are not being inhibited by an unfamiliar situation.

All hand gestures should be of the 'open' variety, indicating an honest, receptive and open-minded attitude. If the forefinger points like a gun-barrel, with the rest of the hand curled as though gripping the stock, it could mean that person is making a strong point, or that they are about to explode. If the other hand is open, they are making a strong point; but if it is clenched, ease back, let them make their point.

A clenched or closed hand gesture denotes a basically shy,

over-cautious nature: someone with a strong desire to keep command of their emotional responses at all times. People who close their hands and demand that you believe them are being deceptive; the same demand accompanied by an open-handed gesture indicates sincerity.

Now let us look at prospective employers. If they are fiddling with any papers that they have lying on their desk, or if their elbows are resting on the desk and their hands are placed on either side of their head, it can be a sign that their mind is already made up and your interview is a mere formality. If you really want the job, you will have to push a little harder in order to impress them; or you can merely give them the chance to end the interview.

A prospective employer who makes gestures towards you with an open palm is interested in what you have to offer and how you are conducting yourself. Good employers will allow for the awkwardness of an interview and such gestures will indicate that they are giving you every chance. Should their hands grasp each other and rest under their chin with the elbows underneath fairly close to each other on the table, you have captured their interest.

Prospective employers may adopt one of several postures: they may point with one hand, or both; use clenched fists to illustrate a point; adopt an open hand approach; or they may lay both hands flat on the table and lean towards you slightly. The first three could mean that you have won the job. If so, the interviewer will probably relax back and invite questions. But that last gesture could indicate that one or more points will have to be made before a successful decision is reached. However, if that last action is accompanied by an indication that the interview is over, the job will not be yours, or, at the very least, you will not be the first choice.

Obviously, all these examples are simple guidelines and have many variations. Often, we do not recognise them for what they are but, when we do, we should be ready to use them to our advantage.

It is equally important to recognise hand gestures in our social life, not just between friends but with family and people we meet in our daily routine. And, just as we can recognise people by their walk, we can learn to associate people with their habitual gestures; but do we understand those gestures?

Boy Meets Girl

The confident lad will show this with his swagger. Equally, his confidence is revealed if his thumbs are tucked into his belt with the palms and fingers pointing downwards, as if emphasizing the genital area. Such a gesture is an obvious invitation to the girl who may raise her hand to her hair, indicating to the boy that she is aware of him but that he is the hunter.

The couple may go for a drink, or to a disco, and the way that they behave and the gestures they make while talking can be more revealing than the words spoken.

He may airily wave his hands around or adopt that super-confident pose of one leg laid across the thigh of the other. If the girl is completely at ease, she may cross one leg over the other and rest her hand between them. The male exhibitionist will fold his hands behind his head; the ill at ease will fiddle with their nails or fingers, or even nibble at them.

Leisure

The way people hold their cigarettes can also be quite revealing. A cigarette held between the middle and third fingers indicates affectation; if held between finger and thumb, inside a cupped hand, it signifies guilt and may indicate someone who will try to bend the rules to his or her satisfaction.

Even the way a glass is held will give a certain amount of information. For instance, when both hands hold the glass it implies a basic sensuality and earthiness. Selfishness may also be present for such folk are independent and usually prefer as much freedom as they can get.

The 'one-handed' drinkers are nearly always of the superficial type and there are many variations on a theme. Those who hold the base of the glass totally enfolded by the hand are more down to earth than those who continually play with the top of the glass. Those who fiddle with the top, run their finger round the rim or continually tap the rim with their fingernail often try to use people and situations to their own advantage although it can also indicate boredom. But if the hand is held completely over the top of the glass, it indicates someone who is deep in thought or who has an inner problem which bothers them.

Once you are aware of gesture as a ploy in behavioural patterns, you can adopt the more positive ones. Try to remember, however, that a complete absence of gesture will be more noticeable and just as revealing as those little movements that, to the trained eye, speak volumes.

Index

Page references in *italics* refer to illustrations

ambition 36, 64, 81–4, 106
angle of harmony *47*, 48
angle of rhythm *47*, 48
annular finger 29–30
Apollo mount 36
arch pattern 107, *107*, 111, 119
auricular finger 31–2
back of the hand 49
  appearance 52–3
  colour 52
  'mouse' mount 53
  texture 52–3
  see also nails
bars 58, 95
body language see gestures
boy meets girl gestures 125
bracelets see rascettes
breaks in lines 58, 76, 96
business
  ability 21–2, 38, 69
  handshakes 122
  interviews 123–4
  success 21–2, 69
careers 81–4, 85–7
  dual careers 66–7, 85–6
  influence of family on 81–2, 85
caring professions 79, 90
chains 96
children line 90
chirognomy 7
  see also shape of hands
chiromancy 7
  see also lines
circles 94
colour
  of hands 52
  of nails 50
communication with hands 7
  see also gestures
composite finger patterns 108, *108*, 112–13
compound finger patterns 108–9, *108*
conic hands 17–18
courage 39, *117*, 118
creative curve 35–6
creativity 35–6, 64, 66, 94
crosses 95

danger, indicators of 69, 79, 90, 94
  see also breaks in lines
dating events 55, 101, *102*, 103–4
dermatoglyphics 7, 8, 105–13, 115–20
digestive disorders 87
dots 58, 93
elementary hands 17–19, *19*
emotions 40–41, 97
  girdle of Venus 87–8
  head line 67
  heart line 77, 79, 80–81
  Simian line 67
empty hands *61*, 62
family
  influence on career 41, 81–2, 85, 89
  life 41, 73, 74–5, 90
  marriage and children lines 90
  ring 89
  ties 89
fate line 81
  dating system 103
  irregular 82–3
  markings on 84
  regular 82–3
  start of 81–2
  terminations 83
finger patterns 105–13
  positioning of 109–13
fingers 23, *24*
  annular finger 29–30
  auricular finger 31–2
  classification of 32–3
  index finger 26–7
  joints 25
  knotting 25
  knuckles 25–6
  length 23
  medius finger 27–9
  patterns of 105–13
  phalanges 26, 27–8, 29, 31
  sensitivity pads 32–3
  setting of 33
  smooth 24–5
  spacing of 33–4
fingertips 32–3
full hands 59, 60
genito-urinary disorders 89
gesture 8

boy meets girl 125
handshakes 121–3
handwriting 121
interviews 123–4
leisure 125–6
girdle of Venus 87–8
golden rule of palmistry 8, 14
graphology *see* handwriting
great triangle *97*, 98
grilles 94
hands *16*, *19*, *20*
  backs of 49–53
  in communication 7
  conic 17–18
  elementary 18–19
  left 56–7
  mixed 21–2
  philosophic 19
  prints of 9, 11–14
  psychic 21
  right 57
  shape of 7, 15–22
  spatulate 20–21
  square 17
  variations of shape 18–22
handshakes 121–3
handwriting 121
happiness 85
head line 63
  appearance 69
  course of 64–6
  duality 66–7
  forks 66
  Simian line 67, 68
  start of 63–4
healing, aptitude for 90
health indicators 9
  heart line 80
  life line 71–6
  line markings 58, 96
  Mercury line 86–7
  nails 49–52
  stars 95
  white lines 99
heart line
  appearance 79–80
  forked 79
  influences 80
  start 77, 79
  variations *78*
holding a glass 125–6
holding cigarettes 125

home life 41, 73, 74–5, 90
humanitarianism *117*, 119
humour 116–18
hypochondria 86–7
illness *see* health indicators
index finger 26–7
inspiration *117*, 119
intellectual capacity 63–9, 94
interviews, gestures in 123–5
intuition 87
islands 58, 96
joints 25
Jupiter mount 36
knotting of joints 25
knuckles 25–6
leadership 44, 116, *117*
leisure, gestures in 125–6
life, approach to 71–6
life expectancy 75–6
life line 71, *72*
   breaks in 76
   course of 73–4
   dating system 101, *102*, 103
   double lines 75
   length 75–6
   start 71–3
   termination of 74–5
   variations in *72*
life-saving cross 98–9
lifestyle, changes in 57
line of intuition 87
lines 7–8
   average hand 62
   dating events using 55,
     101–4
   differences in 58–9
   empty hands *61*, 62
   full hands 59, *60*
   left and right hands 55–7
   markings on 58
little finger *see* auricular
  finger
loop pattern *106*, 110–11,
  116, *117*, 118–19
marks, special 58, 93–9
marriage line 90
medical stigmata 90
medius finger 27–9
memory, retentive *117*, 118
Mercury line 86–7
Mercury mount 38

middle finger *see* medius
  finger
mixed hands 21–2
moons of the nails 49–50
mount of Neptune 40
mount of the Moon 38
mount of Venus 40–41, 47–8
mounts *37*
   Apollo mount 36
   creative curve 35–6
   Jupiter mount 36
   Mercury mount 36, 38
   mount of Neptune 39–40
   mount of the Moon 38
   mount of Venus 40–41,
     47–8
   mouse mount 53
   placement of 41
   Saturn mount 36
   zone of Mars 38–9
music, appreciation of 116,
  117, 118
mystic cross 98
nails 49
   bitten 52
   colour 52
   moons 49–50
   ridging of 52
   shapes *50*, 50–52
   spotting on 52
occult, interest in 87, 98
palm 38–9
palmar mounts *see* mounts
palmar patterns 115–16,
  117, 118–20
palmistry
   Eastern 40, 103–4
   equipment for 12, 14
   golden rule of 8, 14
   study of 7, 8, 14
   uses of 8–9
personality traits 8–9, 59, 60
phalanges 26–9, 31, 44, 47–8
philosophic hands *19*, 19–20
prints
   methods of taking 12–14
   recording extra
     information 11, 13
   uses of 11
protection, sign of 93
psychic hands 21, *21*

the quadrangle 97–8, *97*
Rajah 116, *117*
rascettes 88–9
ring finger *see* annular
  finger
ring of Saturn 88
ring of Solomon 88
Saturn mount 36
sensitivity pads 32–3
serious intent 116, *117*
shape of hands 7, 15–22
Simian line 67, *68*
sixth sense 117, 118–19
skin patterns 7, 8, 105–13,
  115–20
social affairs, interest in 38–9
spatulate hands *20*, 20–21
square hands 17
squares 93–4
stars 95–6
stress *see* white lines
success 96
  in business 21–2, 69
sun line 85–6
tassels 58, 96
tented arch pattern 107,
  107, 111–12, 119
thumbs
   alignment of *46*, 46–7
   angle of 44, *48*, 48
   basal phalange 47–8
   flexibility of 45
   length of 43–4, 46
   observation of 43
   phalange length 44
   setting of 47
   tips of 45
travel indicators 38, 74–5,
  89, 90–91
triangles 94–5
  great triangle *97*, 98
tridents 96
via lascivia 88
vocational guidance 8–9
white lines 99
whorl patterns 106, *106*,
  109–10, 119
wisdom 88
women, health 89
writer's fork 66
zone of Mars 38–9